UNDERSTANDING UNIVERSITY: A GUIDE TO ANOTHER PLANET

UNDERSTANDING UNIVERSITY: A GUIDE TO ANOTHER PLANET

Christine Sinclair

Open University Press

Open University Press
McGraw-Hill Education
McGraw-Hill House
Shoppenhangers Road
Maidenhead
Berkshire
England
SL6 2QL

email: enquiries@openup.co.uk
world wide web: www.openup.co.uk

and Two Penn Plaza, New York, NY 10121-2289, USA

First published 2006

A catalogue record of this book is available from the British Library

ISBN-10: 0 335 21797 4 (pb) 0 335 21798 2 (hb)
ISBN-13: 978 0 335 21797 7 (pb) 978 0 335 21798 4 (hb)

Library of Congress Cataloging-in-Publication Data
CIP data applied for

Typeset by RefineCatch Limited, Bungay, Suffolk
Printed in Poland EU by OZGraf S.A., www.polskabook.pl

Contents

Acknowledgements

The example of an essay written in text and its translation in Figures 2.1 and 2.2 are reproduced with permission from the *Sunday Herald*.

The first extract in Figure 2.5 is from a story entitled 'I Can't Stop Loving Him' published in *Blue Jeans* in April 1979 and is reproduced here with permission from D.C. Thomson & Co Ltd.

The fourth extract in Figure 2.5 is taken from *Customer Relations for the Introduction of Autocheck*, produced by London Buses Training Centre, Camberwell in 1987 and is reproduced here with permission from Transport Trading Ltd and SCOTTSU Consultants Ltd.

The illustrations are by Harriet Buckley.

Activities at university

There are hints and tips in the book about use of language in a range of university activities. These are across several chapters, but the following contents list may be useful.

List of figures

1 Introduction: which planet are we on?

Why this book was written

This book is for all *students* who feel that their *university* is mysterious, strange or alien (for definitions of student and university, see the glossary at the end of this book). You don't *have* to think that university is an alien place to benefit from the book – it's just that a lot of people do think this, at least for a little while. The book should also be useful for people who are thinking of going to university and for people who want to help students to make the most of their time there (teachers, administrators, parents, partners, employers . . .).

I have worked in three different universities – an ancient one, a modern one, and a former polytechnic that became a university in 1992. In each of these universities, many students have come to me for advice on how to study and write. This book draws on their experiences.

One of the main problems students face is the type of language used in universities. When I became aware of this, I decided to become a student again myself: I wanted to find out what it's like to be exposed to a new *academic* language. My own background is in philosophy and education and I chose to study mechanical engineering as a very different type of subject. I studied first at a college and then at a university, going directly into second year. Many students I was meeting in my work at the time were *direct entry* students who found university very different from college. So this book draws on my own recent experiences as a student as well as the experiences of the students I have met over a number of years in different universities.

In particular, the book has been written because I hear the same expressions so often, and in all types of university:

It's like they're speaking a foreign language.

I feel I'm here under false pretences – I don't really belong.

Sometimes it's like being on another planet.

If you're a student who is feeling like this, or a friend of one, then I hope this book will help you to recognize why it happens and how you can respond appropriately. It offers practical suggestions on how to belong to this new world. You will learn how to engage with new language practices, teaching methods and ways of speaking and writing for particular academic subjects. The language of universities is constantly changing along with new ideas and technology – and you will make your own contribution to this process as a person who is taking part in higher education.

The idea of entering another world or another planet does not have to be intimidating; it can be liberating as well. For all students, going to university means meeting people from a wider range of backgrounds than they have previously encountered, opening up all sorts of new experiences and friend-ships. Here are some comments made by students on the richness of their new environment:

Coming from a small private school, I realized that I just hadn't met many people from other social backgrounds before. I met loads of new people and we had a real laugh telling each other stories about our schools.

I'm a mature student, and I thought it would all be clever posh people – and young. But you get all sorts here.

I pure loved it – I met so many weird and wonderful people in my first week, especially the lecturers. I hadn't a clue what they were talking about though.

In a world that can be sometimes bewildering and sometimes exciting, you'll probably benefit from some translations or explanations of what is going on. A bit of mystery is OK – it can be stimulating – but when people start saying they feel as if they're on another planet, then it's time to put up some signposts.

Different ways to use the book

The book can be read in several different ways, to suit different people's prefer-ences for reading. For example, you could read it right through, skip some bits, or find a specific section that is relevant to your purposes. If you use a combination of these methods, the following list of the book's objectives may help you to decide what to do in this case.

It is hoped that the book will help you to:

- find out how powerful and influential people use 'educated' language (Chapter 2);
- recognize the way experts in your subject(s) talk and write (Chapter 3);
- practise listening, reading, speaking and writing in your chosen subject (Chapter 4);
- meet the university's requirements, including passing *assignments* and exams (Chapter 5);
- use appropriate language for your new social life (Chapter 6);
- respond to the changing nature of language, especially with different technology and new media (Chapter 7);
- understand some new words – or new meanings for existing words (Glossary).

The book aims to support everything you are doing *yourself* to achieve the above list. It offers prompts, ideas and comments from people who've already been through it. It does not provide a step-by-step account of everything you'll need to do at university – such a guidebook would not be possible or desirable.

There is a *glossary* at the end of this book. Like a dictionary it has a list of words in alphabetical order, with definitions. This one also contains examples and explanations and is cross-referenced to relevant parts of the book. So if you hear an unfamiliar word during your time at university, you may be able to find a definition here. It certainly won't cover all the potential unfamiliar words, however, and it will help if you find a good quality dictionary too. If a word in the Glossary is used in the book, it is in italics the first time it is used. There are also words in the Glossary that are not used in the book.

In Chapters 2 to 7, the text is broken up with examples, quotations, questions and activities. This is to encourage you to think about what you are reading and to apply it to your own situation. Again, there will be differing responses to this; some people will like to have a notebook and pen at hand, while others won't actually do the activities but may well find themselves thinking about them. The activities include prompts to use when you have a specific task, such as attending a *lecture*, reading a chapter of a book, starting an *essay* or planning your revision.

The quotations are taken from real conversations with students, lecturers, parents and employers. Some of the examples may surprise you and you may find yourself saying: 'Imagine someone not knowing that word!' All the examples are versions of things that people have actually said to me. I have not included any names, and some minor details are changed to be sure that people remain anonymous, but I have 'confessed' to some major areas of ignorance of my own! I should stress, however, that the tone of the book is positive – like many students, I have thoroughly enjoyed all my university experiences, even though I occasionally had some problems understanding what was going on.

In Chapters 6 and 7, a *case study* is used to show how relationships between people and university practices build up over time. Again, this is drawn from an amalgamation of actual language use (though in some cases the people speak a bit more politely here than they did in real life).

As you go through the book, you will 'hear' voices from several places: I've worked at three universities and have degrees from two others; I've undertaken qualifications at three different colleges; I have family and friends at many other institutions. Because of my wide-ranging experience, I hear some comments over and over again, but of course the situation is new to every new student who makes the comment.

I also include extracts from my own *journal* that I kept as a mechanical engineering student in my recent attempt to learn a new academic language. Here is one from early in my course.

> He [the lecturer] asked if we'd followed it so far & I hadn't a clue what was going on. My reasoning was 'no I haven't but it's probably because I missed something last week/at school and so I'll just catch up with it in my own time.'
>
> (extract from Christine's journal)

I remember keeping my face rigid in the hope that my ignorance wouldn't show. Later I began to realize that this was not always a sensible tactic and started to ask some questions. But I also became aware that 'not having a clue' was sometimes inevitable and that things would become clearer with increased exposure to the ideas.

It may comfort you to know that even a lecturer with many years' experience can feel as if she's on another planet!

2   How do they manage to talk like that?

> I just wish I had the 'higher' language. I'd be able to do so much if I could talk the way the people with the higher language talk.
>
> (business student, direct entrant into second year,
after college)

This chapter aims to help you to find and understand the 'higher' language referred to by the business student who came to see me. He had begun to realize at college that certain language practices give people an advantage in both education and work. This is not just to do with accent, speaking 'posh' or using fancy words; it's more about having words and phrases available to express complex ideas. Talking about 'higher' language is itself a complex idea; when he recognized this, my student needed a vocabulary to talk about this language, explore it and eventually to speak it.

Even if you already speak the 'higher' language because of your schooling or family life, it is useful to have some notion about how it works. The history of language itself shows that it is constantly evolving. What is regarded as 'higher', 'educated' or even 'standard' English today may well change over your own lifetime. You can see that I have some reluctance to use these terms – higher, educated and standard – as they are all loaded expressions. I use *scare quotes* (see Glossary) around them sometimes to show that I am not necessarily accepting the implications behind them. In particular, if you do not speak what is thought of as 'educated' language, this does not mean that I regard you as uneducated. (Unfortunately, some people may make such a judgement though.)

There is also a strong association between educated language and power. As a university student you will probably see the advantage of education in being able to recognize and possibly even use sources of power.

In the right places at the right times

The people who use educated language do so because of their own histories. They have been exposed to educated language at home, at school and in their social life. They have been encouraged to read particular types of book, magazine and newspaper, to listen to certain radio and television stations and to enjoy particular types of film, drama and music. Such people have joined in conversations with friends, relations and neighbours who have given them ideas and suggested other books, films etc. that will further influence the way they speak and write.

We all do these things: we read, watch, listen, enjoy entertainment – and then talk to others about what we find interesting or enjoyable. And that way, our language takes on some of the ideas, words and meanings that we discuss with the people we meet. It reaches the stage where we can use a sort of shorthand with friends and relatives. You can see this with in-jokes and the use of catch-phrases from television.

Question 1

Can you think of any expressions you use with your own group of friends, your partner or your family that other people might not understand? Or an expression that you would only know if you'd seen a certain TV programme?

(There are further comments on this question in the Appendix.)

Some of the higher or 'educated' language consists of in-jokes and catch-phrases that depend on a great deal of reading or other sources of cultural knowledge. If you have not been part of the environment, then you will miss the subtle points that are being made.

You used to be able to assume that all students had read *Alice in Wonderland* when they were children, and so you could make reference to some of the reasoning that Lewis Carroll made fun of. You can't any more, so that means we've lost a point of shared reference.

(lecturer in computing)

While the lecturer may regret the loss of this useful source of shared under-standing, he and the rest of us have to accept that language use is always changing. He may need to find alternative sources of shared reference points.

'Educated' language, then, is available to those people who have been ade-quately exposed to it. Schools, colleges and universities can reinforce the edu-cated language practices found in homes and neighbourhoods. Alternatively, they can make students feel that their own language practices are unacceptable or something to be ashamed of – that they are not examples of the 'higher' language that is so valued. You shouldn't feel ashamed if you have not been exposed to something that other people have; it is not your fault, nor an indication that you are 'thick', yet many students feel this way.

Below I briefly explore the reasons for the different types of language use that have evolved. This is not a very deep review; readers who are interested in exploring this issue further should consult the *References* and *Bibliography* at the end of the book.

Changing language: from ancient texts to texting

Much of the work in universities over the centuries has related to the study of *texts*, both ancient and modern. The word 'text' has itself had several meanings that have evolved over the years. Its source is the Latin word for 'weave' (you see this source in words like 'textile' and 'texture' as well). The idea we draw from this is that a text has a *structure* – it consists of a set of words that are woven together in a distinctive form, giving a text recogniz-able features that are appropriate to what it is trying to do (its function). Nowadays, the definition is extended to include sounds and images as well as words.

A 'text' can refer to a physical object – for example, a book or a manuscript. From ancient texts that have been carefully preserved, we have a record of the ideas and language used in a particular time. The physical aspect of texts can be significant, but we are also particularly interested in the language that is used and how that language is structured to express the important ideas of the time.

As technology has changed, so have the texts – the structured use of language – that we have at our disposal. Today, we have texts that can be sent from one mobile phone to another, resulting in a new form of language, texting, that has developed to respond to this new medium.

Text in this sense grew rapidly at the start of the twenty-first century, mainly influenced by the practices of young people sending frequent messages to each other using their mobile phones. When this language then began to influence their other language practices in schools and universities, some older people began to get alarmed, as is illustrated in Figure 2.1. This example is from an essay written by a 13 year old school student. It was quoted in an article in the *Sunday Herald*.

My smmr hols wr CWOT. B4, we usd 2 go 2 NY 2C my bro, his GF & thr 3 :-@ kds FTF. ILNY, its gr8.

Bt my Ps wr so {:-/ BC o 9/11 tht they dcdd 2 stay in SCO & spnd 2wks up N.

Up N, WUCIWUG -- 0. I ws vvv brd in MON. 0 bt baas & ^^^^^.

AAR8, my Ps wr :-) -- they sd ICBW, & tht they wr ha-p 4 the pc&qt...IDTS!! I wntd 2 go hm ASAP, 2C my M8s again.

2day, I cam bk 2 skool. I feel v O:-) BC I hv dn all my hm wrk. Now its BAU ...

Figure 2.1 Concern over the language of texting

Here are two more extracts from the same article:

She [the teacher] said: 'I could not quite believe what I was seeing. The page was riddled with hieroglyphics, many of which I simply could not translate' . . .
    However Sheila Hughes, a senior lecturer in the department of language education at the University of Strathclyde thinks if teenagers express themselves well with the medium it should be embraced . . . 'Pupils have power and control of that language and it has a purpose we have to value.'

It is easy to imagine that many teachers, parents and other readers of the newspaper might have been concerned about the story. Some would even say that it provides *evidence* of low standards. When people make such observations about language, their great fear is that we'll lose communication between generations or between cultures. They are particularly worried that younger people will lose some of the ideas of the older generation, along with the language. This can happen when the words used do not have the range of ideas that can be expressed by a richer language.
    The older generation's *argument* is not an adequate one for getting rid of the language of texting – it would be impossible to prevent the practice anyway. Text has arisen as a language because it is so useful in an age of rapid communication. However, it is not particularly useful for expressing *abstract* academic ideas or exploring subtle differences in meaning.
    The schoolgirl's essay was a rather simple one – it was humorous and to the point, which might be acceptable for an essay on 'What I did in my summer holidays'. The main problem here was that it did not communicate its message to its final reader who required a 'translation' (Figure 2.2). However, this kind of language – even in translation – would not be able to get across the subtle ideas that *academics* look for in writing.

My summer holidays were a complete waste of time. Before, we used to go to New York to see my brother, his girlfriend and their three screaming kids face to face. I love New York, it's a great place.

But my parents were so worried because of the terrorism attack on September 11 that they decided we would stay in Scotland and spend two weeks up north.

Up north, what you see is what you get – nothing. I was extremely bored in the middle of nowhere. Nothing but sheep and mountains.

At any rate, my parents were happy. They said that it could be worse, and that they were happy with the peace and quiet. I don't think so! I wanted to go home as soon as possible, to see my friends again.

Today I came back to school. I feel very saintly because I have done all my homework. Now it's business as usual...

Figure 2.2 Translation of example of texting

Texting also loses one of the valuable features of ancient texts – a permanent record that can be seen by future generations. Human beings are naturally curious about their history; if all our communications are by email, text and other electronic means then we won't leave a trace of ourselves for future generations. At present, there is little danger of this! The paperless office and university don't seem to be very likely.

Key points about texts, then, are:

- they are structured forms of communication, with a particular form;
- they have emerged and evolved for a particular reason;
- they have historical significance.

These points are true whether you are talking about web pages, text messages used on mobile phones, or academic texts used in universities. So what should you be looking out for in academic texts?

A geography student, for example, will inevitably look at maps. These texts have changed considerably over the years and can have many different purposes. The changes in ways we make our representations of the geography of the world reflect changes in the way we think about the world. Different groups of people would put different places in the centre of the world, for instance. Countries have been coloured in different ways to show alliances and empires.

A textbook on a modern language has probably evolved in response both to changes in the language and also changes in our understanding of good ways to teach modern languages. These teaching methods have changed rapidly over recent years, for example with increased emphasis on immersion into the foreign language – that is, speaking it all the time.

A science textbook for today will look very different from one for lessons 100 years ago, yet it will use some of the same ideas and principles as the older book and it would be possible to suggest some links between them. In the seventeenth century, Sir Isaac Newton wrote in a letter: 'If I have seen further it is by standing on the shoulders of giants.' He himself, of course, provided ample shoulders for future generations of scientists.

Question 2

What sort of texts are you likely to study at university? Think about their age, the reasons they have emerged, how they were written or produced. Have they changed over time and are they likely to change much in the near future?

Language and power

In the example of texting in the previous section, we could see how people latched on to the useful features of text messages to communicate with each other in a way that rapidly evolved into a language of its own. People influenced each other very quickly as they passed the idea on to their friends.

The responses from teachers and others who are concerned about language reflect a different type of influence – one that is related to maintaining certain ways of doing things because we need to have standard ways in order to communicate. As I've already suggested, however, standard ways do change.

Changes in texts such as books and maps arise because one way of recording and reflecting our view of the world is preferred to another. The new forms suit the needs of the people who are using them. But who decides what forms the records of the world should take?

Anything that you say or write could be said or written in another way. This is an important point – it will be mentioned again – but it is one that is easy to forget, especially when people are worried about the 'right' way to do something. Clearly then, if something is considered to be written or said the 'right' way, it is because powerful people or groups have decided that this is the case. The power may come from people's ability to express ideas in an appealing way, so that others want to adopt this way. The power may also relate to people's authority or their position in society that allows them to regulate what other people do.

Universities are places where both these sources of power can be seen; that is:

- *scholars* with new exciting ideas have influenced and are influencing the way we see the world and the way we record what we see;

- universities have a long tradition of scrutinizing new ideas rigorously, which means that they regulate the ways in which scholars and students can talk and write about the world.

There is an immediate tension between the first and the second point. Universities are sources of new ways of expressing ourselves but they are also likely to challenge these new ways.

Universities are likely to challenge expressions of ideas for some of the following reasons:

- the ideas do not answer the question they are supposed to;
- they do not take into account the best of the current ideas in the field;
- they do not have a clear line of reasoning;
- they are not presented in the style that has evolved to express academic ideas.

The above list is useful whether we are talking about the new ideas of established scholars, or the essays of students who are trying to come to terms with what is expected of them at university. We will be looking at all of these issues; at present, we are particularly interested in the last one.

Getting exposed to powerful language

Shouldn't we be allowed to speak our own language?
(first year student, business studies)

I have much sympathy with students who ask why their own language is not acceptable at university. In many cases, the lecturer can understand what is meant, even if the student's statement is not grammatically correct according to standard English. However, whether it is fair or not, it is important that students recognize the effects that their speech and especially their written English can have. If you don't speak or write in the appropriate way for the circumstances you are in, then you may find yourself in difficulties. Comedy writers make great use of this, putting people into situations where the way they speak normally does not apply. You also see this in life-swap television programmes, where people are taken from a familiar environment and asked to find their way in another.

Sometimes students are afraid that if they try to sound like 'educated' speakers, they will be ridiculed or in some way 'found out'. There is also a fear of not being accepted by your own family and friends if you start to use language in a different way. These are very real fears and they do have some foundation, which is why I want to acknowledge them before moving on to

---

Question 3

Imagine a very correct older person trying to speak the language of young people in your part of the country. What would they sound like? Would they be able to do it? What would need to happen before they could do it properly?

---

consider what you may have to do to gain the 'higher' language. Perhaps one of the following observations will help you to see where you or your friends are in relation to the kind of language needed to succeed at university.

- People use language differently at different times without really thinking about it. For example, the way you speak will differ if you are at a job interview, at a football match, or at a funeral.
- We do things with language: for example, by using just a few words we can make a promise, get married or launch a ship. Simply by signing a piece of paper, a powerful person can end a war. At university, one of the main things you will do with language is *reason*. The ability to reason requires some language tools of its own.
- If people in power use language to keep their power, it is useful for the other people to be able to know about it and recognize it.

So how do you expose yourself to the language practices that powerful or educated people use? At the start of this chapter, I pointed out that people who are very much at ease with some of these language practices have probably been exposed to them through books, newspapers, television and radio, and cultural activities such as theatre. As our use of different media expands, for example through the *World Wide Web*, so will the sources of powerful use of language.

I try to encourage my students to listen to Radio 4, but I don't think many of them do. It's a pity because some of the current affairs programmes debate issues that we're discussing in class.

(lecturer)

For some students, it may also be necessary to expose yourself to less educated forms of language. For example, if you doing a course in media studies or social work, it may be necessary to see how the 'red top' popular newspapers use language to persuade readers to take a particular perspective.

Some students living away from home, perhaps particularly international students, may find they need to listen to local radio stations to help them to understand local dialects and speech, especially if they are going to have to go on placements.

Question 4: What language do you encounter?

Consider your own exposure to educated and powerful use of English. Is it already quite high? Could it be increased? Think about what happens in the circumstances given in Figure 2.3. Note that it is not being suggested here that you should give up the reading, cultural activities or friends you enjoy! However, it may be possible for you to increase your exposure to some of the alternatives. How far do your answers in the two columns coincide?

	My preferences	'Educated' preferences
Newspaper		
TV channel Type of programme		
Radio channel Type of programme		
Books		
Children's books		
Music		
Discussions with friend		
Internet sites		

Figure 2.3 Preferences in sources of language

Educated language and the language of education

Exposing yourself to educated or powerful language will help you to pick up certain ways of looking at the world and some subtleties in ideas. You will realize that the choice of one word over another does not just affect meaning: it can also change how a reader or listener is influenced by everything else that you say.

Some of the things that will influence an academic reader's or listener's perception of you might be:

- use of correct or incorrect grammar;
- use of the appropriate words from your own subject;
- use of neutral and impersonal language, especially in writing.

An example of grammar use

In certain parts of the country, some frequently used words differ from 'standard English'. A very typical example is the *past participle*. If you have been brought up in a part of the country where people naturally say 'I have wrote', then you may not be aware that some people will regard this as a sign of poor literacy. It is important that you know this; what you do with the knowledge is up to you.

Your essays and *reports* are likely to receive lower grades if you include the wrong past participles in them (the last word in the final column in Figure 2.4). The list in the box in the figure shows you what 'educated' speakers do with past *tenses* and past participles. If you want to be credible with these speakers, you will need to use them in the way that they do.

In some parts of the country, speakers use different forms of past tense and perfect tense from the 'prestige' examples given below. It is important that you know the version that the educated speakers prefer. This may, of course, change at some time in the future; it is likely to remain this way during your time at university, however.

Usually, a past tense and a perfect tense are formed simply by adding -ed to the main verb. Thus we get:

| I play | I played | I have played |
| I want | I wanted | I have wanted |

Quite a substantial number of commonly used verbs do not follow this, however. Here are some that you are likely to need.

Present tense	Past tense	Perfect tense
I am	I was	I have been
I begin	I began	I have begun
I bring	I brought	I have brought
I come	I came	I have come
I do	I did	I have done
I give	I gave	I have given
I go	I went	I have gone
I ring	I rang	I have rung
I run	I ran	I have run
I see	I saw	I have seen
I take	I took	I have taken
I write	I wrote	I have written

Figure 2.4 Irregular verbs

> **Question 5**
>
> Can you think of any local uses of grammar or vocabulary that seem to differ
> from what the 'educated' people say?

Words from your own subject

The language of your subject or *discipline* is considered in the next chapter.
Very early in your course it is likely that you will realize that your discipline has
its own vocabulary. Sometimes this means that you will need to learn new
words; sometimes you will have to use existing words in a different way.

> Suddenly realized was using words like 'beam' and 'shaft' without being
> sure of the distinction.
>
> (extract from Christine's journal)

During my engineering course, I frequently had to go to a dictionary and
rethink words that I already knew. I also started to worry about words like
'heat' and 'temperature' which I now had to think about in a different way. I
needed more precise meanings so that I could talk about what was happening
in an engineering process.

Neutral language

> I hope you tell them never to use 'I' in their reports.
>
> (*lecturer* in engineering)

My reply to this lecturer was that I advise some students, including engineering students, that they should not use 'I'. In general, I also advise them to find
out what is and is not acceptable in their own subjects. In many academic
subjects, though not all, you will find that the writers do not use words such as
'I' or 'you'. So instead of writing: 'I tested the substance', a scientist will write:
'The substance was tested.'

This is not, however, true for all academic subjects. In social work, for
example, there are occasions when students are expected to write reflectively
using 'I', the first *person* (see Glossary under 'person').

In most subjects, the word 'you' would be considered too personal for academic writing. The book that you are currently reading is definitely not written in an academic style. This is because I want to speak directly to you; I am
not trying to remove the personal tone in my writing as I would be in an
academic work.

Question 6: Identifying readers and purposes

In Figure 2.5, there are four pieces of writing. You may notice that two of them are written in more neutral language than the others. There are other observations you might make about the language as well. You're asked to say something about reader, purpose, and writer. Comments on this exercise are at the end of the book.

Conclusion

This chapter has encouraged you to consider your own purposes and audience/readers when you are at university. If you want to speak in the way that is appropriate for university, then you need to find out what is valued by your potential readers and listeners. If you do not already speak and write in that way, you may have to make some adjustments. If you do already speak and write in an 'educated' way, then you may need to adjust your opinions of those who do not. It does not mean that they are uneducated or unintelligent.

The key point is that you will need to use particular types of language for particular purposes. While this chapter has made some general points about language, it is now time to look at more specific uses.

Here are four very different pieces of text. Notice their different use of language. Ask these questions of each (comments at the end of the book):

Who's the reader? What's the purpose? What can you say about the writer?

1

The minute I set eyes on Steven, I fell desperately, hopelessly in love with him. It was bad enough that he was my teacher, but when I found out he was married, it seemed like the end of the world...

They tell me I'll grow out of it, that it's just a crush, and they smile, when I tell them that, this time, it's different.

But it is.

Oh, I realise it's now a new story – love at first sight, a schoolgirl's crush for her teacher. A married man, naturally. And I know it's just one of the hazards an attractive male teacher has to put up with.

But that doesn't make it any less real.

2

Terms of Reference
This report has been commissioned by the General Manager of HAL Computers to explain the need for Quality Assurance during the contract review and design cycle. Problems have arisen during this phase for the new compact electrical power supply unit for the current PC.

Outline Methodology
Quality Assurance differs from quality inspection by 'building quality into the product in the first place' (Deming, 1986). This means that the design phase of a new product or component is critical. The design must meet the requirements of the customer and it must also be possible to implement the design at an appropriate cost.

3

In particular, a contrast has been drawn between Leont'ev's material view of activity and Vygotsky's emphasis on how signs (such as words) mediate human activity (Kozulin, 1996). Again, we see that the emphasis changes depending on the specific writer's unit for analysis (Daniels, 2001:85). Thus Wertsch's (1991) unit for analysis is mediated action and Engeström's (2002) is the activity system (or even the interaction between activity systems). There are also synergies: Wells' (1999) unit for analysis is dialogue and he builds a framework to explore this from Vygotsky's ZPD, activity theory, and Hallidayan notions of register and genre.

4

positive effects of a faster system

As we've already said, the main advantage to you from the new system will be speeding up the boarding process. This should be better for you because it will result in:

• fewer complaints from customers
• more customers, therefore more revenue for the company
• less frustration for you
• less time spent checking passes
• more job satisfaction

(You may have come up with other positive effects in your answers to some of the activities.)

However, progress can also bring problems.

Figure 2.5 Four texts

3   Joining an academic tribe

An academic *researcher* and writer, Tony Becher, coined the phrase *'academic tribes* and territories' and gave this title to a book he wrote in 1989. In this book, he pointed out that each subject area (or academic discipline as it is sometimes called) has its own way of doing things. For example, if you are studying several very different subjects, you may notice that staff tend to be more formal in one than in another. You may also notice that the textbooks are written very differently.

Unless they have read Becher's (1989) book, academic staff would probably not know what you are talking about if you refer to an academic 'tribe'. They will talk rather about 'subject' or 'discipline'. But I like the *metaphor* of 'tribe' and it fits into the idea of another planet, so I use it frequently in this book. It draws attention to the fact that language is used in different ways in different subjects.

Question 7: The language of your textbooks

Take two textbooks that you will be using this year, ideally as different as possible. See whether you can answer the questions in Figure 3.1.

Once you have done Question 7, you might find yourself thinking about the way language is used in your chosen 'tribes' and whether you are going to feel comfortable with this language. Remember that even though the new language can be uncomfortable at first, you may eventually get used to it.

	Book A	Book B
Is it going to be easy to read? Why?		
Is the language formal or informal? What examples show this?		
Does the book seem to value: – clear argument? – real-life examples? – illustrations? – problem and solutions? – theories? – other?		
Does the book have an *index* at the back? Are there words in this that you don't know yet?		
What does the contents page tell you about the way the book is organized? (e.g. does it build up a story, deal with several separate issues, move from simple to complex ideas?)		
What other features are there in the language of these books?		

Figure 3.1 Textbook language

The language of your subject

Figure 3.2 shows some personal observations on the language of some of the subjects I have studied in further and higher education. In the figure, you can see that the language difficulties I encountered varied with the subjects I studied and were also frequently tied in with my earlier experience. I particularly found this with English literature – a subject I excelled in at school and struggled with in my first year at university.

While the examples in Figure 3.2 show that there are some differences between subjects, some general observations can also be drawn:

- It's a good idea to look for a specialist dictionary/encyclopaedia or other reference book that gives simple explanations of the key ideas in your subject.
- New words may be uncomfortable at first, but you will probably eventually get used to them.
- Existing knowledge may sometimes be inappropriate for the new circumstances.
- Things may be done differently at university from school or college.

This last point is worth exploring in more depth.

Philosophy	There were quite a few words that ended in '-ology' – epistemology, ontology, teleology. I kept confusing them. In the library, I found a philosophical encyclopaedia that gave me short accounts of different topics – I didn't find it until my third year though and it would have been very useful in my first year!
English literature	The literature I was reading was much harder to follow than the literature I'd enjoyed at school. I certainly needed the lectures and commentaries to guide me to what I should be looking at. There was one lecturer who always marked me down, but I never understood what I was doing wrong.
German	The main thing I remember about studying German was that I tried to be too smart. I'd been in Berlin for an exchange visit and had picked up some slang which I used in one of my essays. The lecturer didn't understand it and I don't think it went down too well.
Education	I first studied 'educational technology', which was itself a confusing title, referring more to methods than to equipment. There seemed to be a lot of *jargon* in education that used ordinary words in a specific way, such as 'objective' and 'evaluation'. I didn't like some of these uses at first; eventually I found them useful shortcuts. But I remained concerned sometimes if I thought language was being used to constrain what it was possible to do in schools and universities...
Language and literacy	... and when I studied language and literacy as part of a *Masters* in education I realized that language does reflect the powerful relationships in society. But the language of language and literacy is itself complex – the word 'discourse' especially seemed very hard to pin down and was used in different ways by different writers.
Mechanical engineering	I got into a few muddles with new words, old words with new meanings, abbreviations and symbols. I realized how important it was to be precise about quantity – it was too easy to be out in calculations by a factor of a million! If I could recognize what the figures were actually telling me, this was less likely.

Figure 3.2 Language issues in different subjects

How a subject changes from school or college

I intended doing a degree in English literature; it was my best subject at school. I continued to do well in my first *semester*, but my marks went right down in the second semester. Years later, I thought that perhaps I was not as in tune with the English department's ways as I might have been. It seemed very different from school.

(philosophy *graduate*)

I was the English literature student in the quotation above. Though my marks went back up again, I was unable to continue with my chosen preference for honours and switched to doing honours philosophy instead. For a long time, I said that this had happened because I had a known 'tough' marker in my second semester. While there may be some truth in this, it still would have helped if I had had some better insight into what was required and expected by English lecturers at university. With philosophy – a new subject – I had to work this out anyway. Because I had always been 'good' at English, I thought I knew what was needed in this new environment. Being already good in the subject possibly got in the way of making appropriate adjustments.

Here are some other students' observations on this phenomenon:

At college, I always got merits so I thought I must be quite good. Here, even when we're supposed to be covering the same topic, there are huge differences and I'm not getting good marks at all. I'm really good at getting hold of the information, but I now realize that there's always an angle on the question and I need to make sure I follow that. It's taken me a whole semester to learn this. It would have been helpful if someone could have warned me.

(third year social sciences student, direct entrant with HND)

I was OK at first – we seemed to be going over the same biology as I'd done the previous year at school. But the way we had to write up our findings for our lab report was completely different and that threw me. I thought they'd go over it but they didn't. They said it was in the *handbook*. I didn't read the handbook so I just did it the way we'd done it in school. Apparently that wasn't what they wanted. I think they should show you for your first one.

(first year science student)

Don't assume that they will show you. And it's always a good idea to look at the handbook (if you have been given one) before starting an assignment.

Staff have noticed some of the differences between school and university too.

Even when I've demonstrated to them that their assumptions are wrong, I still get students refusing to change what they do because 'this is the way we were taught at school'.

(*professor* of mathematics)

There are a number of lessons that can be taken from the experiences of these students and staff:

- Your academic 'tribe' may operate differently at university; this not just a case of more advanced study; it may be a whole new approach.
- Some of the ways you've always used may not be appropriate for the current circumstances; this can be a very hard lesson.
- Eventually, if you really feel that you are not going to be able to fit in to the way your chosen tribe works, you might want to consider switching to another one. (This is a big decision and not one to be taken too hastily; however, in many universities where there is an option to switch, the sooner you can do it the better.)

One of the big differences at university is that it can take some time before you know how you're fitting in with the language. While at school or college you might get some *feedback* on what you say or write in the first few weeks, at university students can still be left wondering how they are coping six weeks into the term. In some university courses it can be even longer before students are told how they are doing.

I have often noticed an increase in the levels of anxiety in students about one to two months into a course, and I think this is connected with uncertainty over whether this subject is 'for me'. For some students, this problem is just a matter of doing what has to be done to get by; a few eventually feel that they have to remove themselves from the situation. If you are one of the latter, you should seek advice from your department about the appropriate way of doing it.

However you feel about it, in order to progress to the higher levels of your chosen subject, you are going to have to learn its vocabulary, its symbols and its shorthand expressions.

New words and new meanings

I kept hearing the word 'oscillate'. I just hadn't heard it before I went to university.

(first year medical student)

In our first tutorial, we were asked, 'Are moral judgements subjective?' I had a wide vocabulary but I didn't know what 'subjective' meant. It got a lot worse later when another student in the class started talking about 'hegemony'. I was completely lost.

(philosophy graduate)

Here are some dictionary definitions of those problem words:

hegemony . . . preponderant influence, esp. of one state over others . . .
oscillate   . . . to vary between certain limits . . .
subjective . . . influenced by or derived from personal taste or opinion
                and lacking impartiality or objectivity . . .

(Chambers Dictionary, 2003)

The three dots (. . .) in the definitions indicate that there are other words that I have missed from the Chambers' definitions. I have selected the definition most suitable for the situation the students were in – their context. Other definitions, such as '**subjective** . . . nominative (*gram*) . . .' would not have been appropriate for the context and would possibly not have been understood by the student anyway. So while the dictionary is useful for getting an initial idea of what is going on – and you're certainly advised to get one and use it – you might have to make a selection.

You might not get as full a picture as you need. The medical student learned more about oscillation through seeing examples and becoming aware of effects than she might have from the dictionary. I learned what 'subjective' meant during the tutorial where we argued about whether there was a need to have shared ideas of right and wrong. Using a dictionary helps to prepare the mind; it is not the end of the story.

During my recent engineering course, I came across several new words, such as 'enthalpy' and 'interferometry'. These were two that caused me a lot of problems. I had to understand the processes that the single word was summarizing. I had to first hear or read the word and know that there was a process; then I had to be exposed to a number of examples relating to that process. So it is important to recognize that *it can take time to understand a new word* – that you need to be exposed to it in a number of different contexts. Many students get distressed with new words, particularly if they are faced with a lot of them at once. I would argue that this distress can even be part of the learning process for some people.

Sometimes a word you've always used in a particular way has to change its meaning for your new context. A very common example of this is 'argument'. Students are told that their essays have to contain an argument; for some, this sounds too much like a fight and they don't want to do that. Here are just some of the dictionary definitions of 'argument'. Some do relate to essay writing, some to problem-solving – and they do not all have the idea of an aggressive approach.

argument a reason or series of reasons offered or available as proof or inducement (with *for* or *against*); exchange of such reasons; debate; matter of debate or contention; an unfriendly discussion; a summary of subject matter; . . . a variable upon which another depends, or a quantity or element to which a function, operation etc. applies (*maths, comput, logic*); the angle between a vector and its axis of reference (*maths*).

(*Chambers Dictionary*, 2003)

You may recognize from this series of definitions that an essay requires a good line of reasoning, rather than an unfriendly discussion. Again, you will need to be further exposed to the idea of an academic argument before you can fully understand what is meant by 'argument', and we'll return to this topic later (Chapter 5). You will also see from the above definitions that mathematicians have their own understandings of what 'argument' could mean.

Some words, then, are representations of a situation or process. Their precise meaning may take some time to understand. This is also true of shorthand for words and expressions and you will inevitably meet some examples of these as well.

Signs and symbols

You say, 'What's that squiggly thing?' and they go, 'Oh, that's sigma.' Yeah, RIGHT.

(first year student)

Signs and symbols are frequently used as shorthand for complex ideas or instructions. When you do recognize them, then it can be hard to see them as shorthand; you just follow the instruction. When you were learning to add and subtract, you first had to learn that + means 'add the numbers on either side' and − means 'take the number after the sign from the number before it'. It takes too long to write it out in full, and it's hard to read too. The plus or minus sign is much easier. So now it's just automatic.

There may be some other signs that you will need to know as 'automatically' as + or −. If you know that you are weak in this, it is worth going over notes from school or college or looking at some of the texts you are going to be studying at university to see whether they contain any signs and symbols you ought to understand but do not. (In some new subjects, you may not be expected to know the symbols already, but it's still worth looking out for them.)

If you are studying any subject with a mathematical basis, you will need to know the Greek alphabet. Figure 3.3 shows the Greek alphabet, showing both

A	α	alpha		N	ν	nu
B	β	beta		Ξ	ξ	xi
Γ	γ	gamma		O	o	omicron
Δ	δ	delta		Π	π	pi
E	ε	epsilon		P	ρ	rho
Z	ζ	zeta		Σ	σ	sigma
H	η	eta		T	τ	tau
Θ	θ	theta		Y	υ	upsilon
I	ι	iota		Φ	φ	phi
K	κ	kappa		X	χ	chi
Λ	λ	lambda		Ψ	ψ	psi
M	μ	mu		Ω	ω	omega

Figure 3.3 The Greek alphabet

capital and lower case letters. If your lecturer says a word like 'sigma' or 'delta' and makes a squiggle on the board, then check the figure to see if one of the Greek letters is involved.

Once you recognize the Greek letters, you will be able to learn a precise meaning for them. The letters become symbols for important expressions. For example, the 'squiggly thing' referred to by my student – capital sigma (Σ) – is used to indicate that you need to add up the numbers given. It is also known as the summation sign. This is very obvious *if you already know it*; if you don't, then of course it's like another language. That's what it is. And, as we've seen above, there are two stages of translation: the Greek letter and the squeezing of a complex idea into a single symbol.

Because some of these letters are similar to English ones, they can be confusing and difficult to write. It can be hard to distinguish the lower case rho (ρ) from an English p, for example. It helps if you slant it a bit.

Question 8

Have you forgotten any important expressions represented by the Greek letters in Figure 3.3? Might you need them for your university course?

Other shorthand expressions: jargon, abbreviations and acronyms

One of the problems students have with 'higher' language is that there is so much jargon. This word 'jargon' is often used very negatively, and its definitions do include 'gibberish' and 'twittering' (*Chambers Dictionary*, 2003). But like the signs and symbols already considered, it does actually have a use in providing shorthand meanings for professions or subjects. A lawyer uses a legal term with a very precise meaning to discuss a case with another lawyer. If they did not have this shared meaning, then it would take them even longer to talk about the topic.

The reason jargon is so hated is that it can also be used to exclude people who are not 'in the know'. Once a person has become very familiar with the jargon word, then it can slip into everyday speech and annoy people who don't know the word. It is undoubtedly true that some people will use jargon or 'higher' language just to try to create a good impression, rather than to be really clear or precise.

As a new student, you will need to learn the jargon of your own subject, especially when it includes words with a precise meaning that are needed for the type of shorthand you'll be using with lecturers and fellow students. Because it can take time to understand fully the meaning of a new idea, you maybe won't know for a while which words are going to be the important ones. It is quite possible that you will be one of those people who is annoyed by jargon before you can move on to being one of those who can see the point of it.

Jargon often comes in the form of abbreviations and *acronyms*, which can be very intimidating if you don't know what they mean. An acronym is just an abbreviation that forms another word – for example, 'radar' is an acronym for 'radio detection and ranging'; 'NATO' or 'Nato' is an acronym for the 'North Atlantic Treaty Organization'.

While 'radar' and 'NATO' have become part of everyday vocabulary, many examples of abbreviations and acronyms have not. A good writer will spell out the abbreviation in full on the first use of it, and may even include a glossary of terms. You will find yourself quickly using abbreviations that are common to your own subject area and it is important to remember that you need to explain them to non-experts and on occasions when you have to pretend that your lecturer is a non-expert.

There are some abbreviations that you must have at your fingertips if you are going to perform calculations and measurements. These include the SI units (Système International d'Unités) based on the metre, kilogramme and other principal units. I got into a mess with these in my engineering course and sometimes found myself out in my calculations by a factor of a thousand or a million! This would be very dangerous for a practising engineer. While I was trying to sort it out, I ran into another problem with abbreviations:

However, the question on the sheet has atmospheric pressure in mmHg and I still don't know what that means.

mm = millimetre = m/1000.

Hg =?

(extract from Christine's journal)

If you do understand this, you will probably be very amused at my ignorance. I was certainly embarrassed about it afterwards. I knew from chemistry at school that Hg was the abbreviation for mercury and I also knew that mercury is used in measuring atmospheric pressure. But because I was trying to sort out my SI units, I thought that mmHg represented some kind of measure (involving both millimetres and grammes). I temporarily 'lost' my existing knowledge because I was distracted by some units I was unsure of. I only tell you this to let you know that it can happen!

To avoid this situation, make sure you are on top of the abbreviations used in connection with SI units (see Figure 3.4). If appropriate to your study, you will also want to refresh your memory on the table of chemical elements.

Figure 3.4 shows that a kilometre (km) is 1000 metres (a metre multiplied by 10^3) and a millimetre (mm) is a thousandth of a metre (a metre multiplied by 10^{-3}). A good dictionary contains this type of information. If you are studying a science subject, it would be a good idea to get a scientific dictionary. Make sure that you will have easy access to definitions that you are likely to need frequently during your course.

Symbol	Prefix	Multiply by
T	tera	10^{12}
G	giga	10^{9}
M	mega	10^{6}
k	kilo	10^{3}
h	hecto	10^{2}
da	deka	10^{1}
d	deci	10^{1}
c	centi	10^{2}
m	milli	10^{3}
l	micro	10^{6}
n	nano	10^{9}
p	pico	10^{12}
f	femto	10^{15}
a	atto	10^{18}

Figure 3.4 Abbreviations used in SI units

Conclusion

In your academic subjects, you'll be faced with new words, new meanings for old words, signs and symbols, jargon, abbreviations and acronyms. For some specialist areas there may be other types of sounds and images not covered here. The important messages from this chapter are:

• many of the new ideas you'll meet in your subjects are condensed so that experts can talk about them easily;

- for complex and condensed ideas and processes, it is unlikely that you will fully grasp the meaning when you first encounter the word;
- dictionaries and other reference books are helpful in preparing your mind, but you must experience the word in an appropriate context to understand its meaning(s);
- some symbols may have to be learned in two stages – e.g. the Greek alphabet and the specific meanings given to a particular letter (there may be several of these);
- above all, you should remember that you will be doing things with these words and other signs – doing things that help you to become a member of a particular academic tribe.

During your course, it may help you to keep a notebook just for unfamiliar words or uses of words and keep trying to refine your definitions and understandings of these words. This could eventually become a useful revision tool.

4 Take me to your leader! How to find out about the tribe

Once you've recognized that your chosen academic tribe has its own language, you'll need an interpreter. Lecturers are the best people to help with this, though they would not necessarily describe their role in these terms.

Lecturers come in the full range of personality types, so you'll inevitably find you get on better with some than others. Even the ones you like a lot are unlikely to provide you with all you need. You'll have to supplement your knowledge about the new language from other sources such as reading and trying things out (e.g. solving problems).

Some of the other sources of information are the 'invisible' members of your academic tribe – those from other institutions, other countries and other times who have written extensively about the problems that interest your tribe.

There are prompts in this chapter to help you to think about responding both to lecturers and to other sources of learning. Towards the end of the chapter, we also look at how the lecturer fits into the rest of the institution.

The lecturer as guru or guide

Traditionally, the lecturer was simply a person who delivered a lecture on an academic topic. Some lecturers still see that as their role: they will give out information and it is up to the student to respond appropriately. However, most lecturers now recognize that they have a 'teaching' function as well, which means that they will be thinking about the students' responses as well as their own delivery.

Lecturers have their post because of their expertise in the subject, which includes knowing how to use its language. One of the problems associated with this is that they may have forgotten what it is like not to know the language: to them it's 'obvious'. When this happens, they may say things that you don't understand but will themselves be completely unaware that they are not communicating.

In one way this is good, because by using the language of the subject and exposing you to it repeatedly, lecturers will help you to see how the language works. Sometimes you'll only realize what's important about an expression when you see it from another angle, and it may be that clarity comes from another student or from something you read. It could be that one lecturer helps you to understand the language used by another.

So lecturers are the sources of knowledge about a subject but they can also act as guides to that knowledge and the language it uses. They will do this in different ways, for example by:

- demonstrating how to do something;
- explaining each step of a procedure;
- pointing out a pattern;
- helping you to see a familiar situation in a new light;
- asking you questions and giving feedback on your answers;
- exposing your misunderstandings and correcting them;
- telling a story about the way things happen in the subject;
- telling you how things are done in the practice of your subject.

These are just some of the actions that might be happening in a lecture, and it is clear from this that lecturing is therefore more than just giving students a list of 'facts' and expecting them to remember them (that may happen as well, of course). There may be several of these actions happening with respect to one topic, and that will be particularly useful because each approach will reinforce the points in a different way. Here's an extract from my journal that illustrates how language becomes clearer with repetition in new contexts.

> Learned a very simple thing from yesterday that seems ridiculous not to have pursued before but I didn't know where to start. Last year I simply did not understand the steam tables. Abbreviations got in the way again h_g = enthalpy of a gas and h_f means enthalpy of a fluid. The diagram we used for refrigeration explains it all.
>
> (extract from Christine's journal)

I had managed to do something using the steam tables without properly realizing what I was doing. The understanding only came when I met the ideas in a new context later, when a different lecturer approached a related topic in a slightly different way. You can't expect to know something fully the first time you encounter it. This means that you should expose yourself to new contexts as much as possible, for example by reading after a lecture or by talking to other students. Don't be afraid to use dictionaries to look up difficult words after a lecture. Many subjects have their own dictionaries, but even then, the precise context of your class may change the actual meaning of the word or symbol. (Ask the librarians in your university for help in finding dictionaries for your subject; you probably won't be able to take them out of the library though.)

The following section looks at these issues in practice, thinking about what might happen in classrooms and how you can make the best response to it.

What lecturers might do in classrooms – and how to respond

University activities 1. Lectures

> My lecturer somehow makes it all interesting. He loves his subject and he's a bit manic sometimes and you've got to pay attention 'cause he'll suddenly ask for a show of hands about something.
>
> (third year student)

This is what many students think lectures should be like – a teacher sharing the love of a subject with the students and treating it as a kind of dialogue. Don't be surprised if you find the lecturer suddenly asks you to do something; this sort of approach is now encouraged in training courses for new lecturers. In some classes, lecturers even have equipment where you can press a button with an answer to a question, like 'Ask the Audience' on the UK TV programme *Who Wants To Be a Millionaire?* This is sometimes known is a *personal response system* (PRS) and it helps the lecturer and the students to see how their understanding is developing.

> At college you could interrupt the lecturer if you didn't understand; it's different here – there are 200 students in the class and it's quite intimidating. And the lecturer doesn't encourage you to say anything.
>
> (student entering university directly into third year with an HND)

Not all lecturers like an interactive style and students who are used to an informal chatty approach may get a shock when they go to a different type of institution. Sometimes it's clear that you're expected just to sit quietly and take notes. In a class of 200, it's hard to ask a question. But it is a good idea to write that question down so that you can look up the answer later on in the library.

I don't know why I bother coming here. I could stay at home and get my girlfriend to read the textbook to me – that's all that lecturer does.

(second year part-time student)

The word 'lecture' comes from the Latin for 'reading' and it is still possible to find lecturers who simply read out a bit of a textbook. Most students find it difficult to respond to this; words written for reading are usually quite hard to follow when they are read aloud. This type of teaching is not effective, but at least you know that if you miss any key points, you should be able to find the textbook and read it for yourself.

I couldn't believe how much you pick up at lectures. She told us there was a mistake in the notes – I wouldn't have known that. She also said things that helped me think about what might come up in the exam. This year, I'm definitely going to all of my lectures.

(student repeating second year)

Sometimes students don't see the point of lectures, especially if the notes are available somewhere else, for example it is often possible to download them from a departmental website or *virtual learning environment* (see Chapter 7 and Glossary). While these can be useful, there is a difference in the quality of the information gained from being present in the classroom – hearing and/or seeing the lecturer. It's also amazing how much the apparently casual remarks some-one makes can suddenly bring a point home to you. When a lecturer reminds the class about a class test, there are always a few people who say: 'What class test?' If they hadn't been at the lecture, they'd have missed something import-ant. You also might pick up useful information from the casual chat with another student after a lecture.

Picking up important things from lectures is easier if you have primed your mind beforehand. Once your lectures have started, you might find the first form in Figure 4.1 helpful to look at before each one. After that, there is a form to prompt you to think about what you need to do *after* the lecture. These forms will not take long to fill in or just think about, but they will help to ensure that the lecture is properly integrated into your understanding. They also make it clear that both lecturers and students have different approaches to lectures and that the choices you make should be tied to the most appropriate purpose or goal.

How you make notes during a lecture is up to you. There is no single right way; there is nothing you 'ought' to be doing. New students often worry about these things. The best way for you to make notes is the one that suits your own style and own purposes. You may still have to find out what this is, however.

Here are some tips about the language of lectures that some students have found useful:

1 Make life easier for yourself later by clearly heading up the lecture with a title, date and the lecturer's name and by numbering all your pages.
2 Keep a wide margin for adding comments, question marks, additional information (often a lecturer will refer back to something).
3 Listen for 'signposts': e.g. 'I am going to talk about *three* topics today.' These will help you to structure the information.
4 Write down words or phrases you don't understand to look up later.
5 If you miss something, note that there's a gap and try to fill it in later.
6 Experiment with different styles, colours and layouts.
7 See the Glossary for a definition and example of '*mindmap*'.
8 If you've never made notes before, try practising by watching (and recording) a documentary on TV; play it back a week later and see if your notes have been a good summary of it.
9 If anything puzzles you during the lecture, turn it into a question.
10 If you have a particular need to tape-record lectures, it is a good idea to ask permission first.

Students with particular needs may have to let the lecturer know before they attend any lectures. For example, it may be necessary to sit near the front or to ask the lecturer to wear a microphone. Disability services can advise on approaching lecturers and perhaps provide a letter or form to alert them of your needs.

University activities 2. Seminars and tutorials

In some institutions or subject areas, there is a clear distinction between *seminars* and *tutorials*. A seminar is a discussion group, often led by a *paper* from one of the students. A tutorial is a small intensive session with just one or two students and a lecturer. Nowadays, however, the two terms are frequently used interchangeably to refer to a discussion group.

You should think of seminars and tutorials as opportunities to go into a topic in greater depth, and particularly for you and other students to be able to talk about the topic. Seminars and tutorials should not turn into mini lectures, but this can happen if the students have not done any preparation or are too intimidated to speak up in front of other people.

> We were told to prepare a case study for our seminar. We didn't know what a case study was and we were worried that we'd look stupid. We thought we ought to know. But we went and asked the study skills adviser and she helped us to see that all we were expected to do was read the material and try to answer some questions. We were well prepared for the seminar and it went well. I enjoyed it.
>
> (student entering university directly into third year with an HND)

It was not the students' fault that they had never come across the idea of a case

The next lecture

Preparing for a lecture can increase your understanding. What do you know now about your next lecture? You might need to do some reading to help you answer some of these questions.

Will the next lecture follow on from an earlier one? If so, where will it pick up?

What is the lecture's theme?

What do you already know about this topic?

What questions might the lecture answer?

When might you have to use the information from the lecture?

Essay/report ☐   Problem ☐   *Project* ☐
Presentation ☐   Exam ☐   Other ☐

What kind of notes will you make during the lecture?

Key words ☐   Headings ☐   Questions ☐
Phrases ☐   Mindmap ☐   Other ☐

After the lecture

What information can you fill in about the last lecture you attended? If you can't answer these questions, should you be able to? If so, what do you need to do?

Lecturer's approach

Was the lecturer trying to provide any of the following?

Introduction to subject area ☐   Overview of a topic ☐
Detailed account of a topic ☐   Framework ☐
Review of known material ☐   Stimulus to find out more ☐
Challenge to preconceptions ☐   Other ☐

Figure 4.1 *continues*

What were the main themes of the lecture?

Were there any aspects of the lecture you didn't understand?

When might you have to use the information from the lecture?

Essay/report	☐	Problem	☐	Project	☐
Presentation	☐	Exam	☐	Other	☐

What will you do now with your notes?

Rewrite	☐	Create mindmap	☐	Highlight	☐
Summarize	☐	File	☐	Other	☐

Figure 4.1 Lecture prompts

study before. I was their study skills adviser and I wasn't too sure how to respond when they asked if I could provide a 'model' for what they should do. It was a good question, though: it is easier to do something when it has been modelled for you. However, there were too many possibilities for what was expected from a case study (see Glossary) and I concentrated on what they were being actually asked to do. This turned out to be simpler than they had thought.

Seminars and tutorials have always been full of students who don't want to say anything for fear of being thought stupid. But when other students feel this too, you may be doing them a favour:

> At the break, he said he felt he was the dunce asking all the questions but his neighbour said: 'No, good on you, mate. I don't have the bottle.'
> (extract from Christine's journal)

If you're going to have the 'bottle' or bravery to talk in a seminar or tutorial, you'll need to do some preparation. It is also very useful to reflect on it afterwards. One of your reflections might be that you were wrong in what you said, but you could only find this out by saying it! The prompts in Figure 4.2 encourage you to think before and after you have attended a seminar.

University activities 3. workshops and labs

Practical sessions where you do an experiment or practise a procedure are an integral part of some courses. Often students enjoy these sessions most because they can see the relevance of what they are learning. But there will be language issues here too, and some of them can be hidden.

Here is an extract from a problem I had 'seeing' what was going on during an experiment involving measurement of light.

The next seminar or tutorial

Group discussions help to reinforce points made during lectures and in books. You'll get most benefit from them if you can participate, at least by understanding what is going on but preferably by joining in any discussion or other activity. Some preparation beforehand will help this.

What is the theme of the seminar or tutorial?

What questions do you have about this topic?

Will the discussion be related to any lectures you've attended?

What words that cause you difficulties might be used in the session?

What should you have read before the seminar or tutorial?

When are you going to read this?

Do you have to write or present anything for this session?

What will be your main activity during the session?

Listening to a mini lecture	☐	Reading	☐
Problem-solving	☐	Talking	☐
Writing	☐	Presenting	☐
Questioning	☐	Revision	☐
Other	☐		

After the seminar or tutorial

Employ the useful words what, where, when, why, how and who to help you to analyse the session. These are also good questions to ask whenever you are stuck, for example with an essay. You might want to add some more questions of your own.

1 What?
What was the subject?
What did you do and say?
What were the main points of the session?
What did you particularly like/dislike about the session?
What did you not understand?
What do you know now that you did not know before?

2 Why?
Why is the subject important?
Why did the lecturer/tutor organize it this way?

Figure 4.2 *continues*

3 When?

When was the session?
When will you use what you talked about?

4 How?

How was the issue unpacked?
How will you use what you talked about?
How did people talk? E.g. did they use everyday examples?

5 Where?

Where was it held?
Where did the discussion lead you?

6 Who?

Who was there?
Who are the important writers for this subject?
Who is most affected by this subject?

Figure 4.2 Seminar prompts

> My problem seems to be that there are too many steps to this process –
> some related to the final condition required for the measurement and some
> relating to what you need to do to produce light that is in this condition.
> (extract from Christine's journal)

In fact, my 'real' problem was that I had simply not been adequately exposed
to the meanings associated with the equipment and the procedure. We were all
crowded round the equipment and I was unable to see each step of the procedure. The notes were very complicated and seemed to bear no resemblance
to what I could see. There did not seem to be much happening – but I could
not see anything happening. To 'see' it, you had to be able to understand some
of the relationships caused by 'interference' – a concept that I had not fully
understood.

There are a number of issues in this example:

- you may need to see something several times from several angles;
- seeing might not be enough; you may need to hear about it too;
- if you cannot see what is going on, you should let the lecturer know;
- if you can use the equipment for yourself, it may be better than just watching
  someone else use it;
- you will benefit from opportunities to talk about what's happening in a lab;
- you will benefit from reading about practical applications of what you are
  seeing in a lab.

The equipment has been developed in response to much *theory* and scientific practice that has evolved over many years and involved much dialogue;
you can't expect just to 'know' that dialogue on your first encounter with the
equipment. So don't think you're stupid just because you don't understand
something the first time you see it!

The other language issue is that you are usually expected to write up your observations of what has happened in a lab or workshop. You will need to ensure that you know what this means in your discipline and in this institution; the approach you took at school or college may not be adequate for university, for example. Don't just assume you know what's wanted – find out. Think about the issues identified in Figure 4.3; do you know the answers to these questions?

The next workshop or lab

Many courses have practical sessions that involve you in experimentation using equipment or trying out a procedure or technique. Though there are many different formats for such sessions, the following questions may be useful prompts before, during and after the session (especially if you're wondering what you should be saying about it!) Listen out for the answers to these questions when the lecturer (or *demonstrator*) tells you about the workshop or lab.

What is the session trying to achieve?

What equipment is involved?

Which people are involved?

What should the experimenter do?

What should the experimenter not do?

Are there any associated health and safety requirements?

What can be seen during the activity?

What can be heard during the activity?

What other senses are involved in the activity?

How does the activity relate to everyday experience?

What does the literature (e.g. recommended reading) say happens during this activity?

What is the required format for reporting this activity? (e.g. is it a talk or a short written report, how long should it be, what headings are required?)

Where are the *regulations*/recommendations for producing this report? (e.g. are they available from the departmental office or from the lecturer?)

Figure 4.3 Workshop and lab prompts

Other activities

Lectures, seminars, tutorials, labs and workshops are all activities that will help you to understand the language and practices of your subject. They will probably be arranged and run by lecturers (or possibly teaching assistants). There are other activities that lecturers might direct you towards, but where they take more of a back seat. In these cases, the lecturers may still advise you on what's appropriate, but they'll expect you to do a lot of work for yourself. Three of these are considered below: reading, problem-solving, and placements.

University activities 4. Reading

> Some lecturers are very lazy. They expect you to look things up for yourselves!
>
> (first year student)

And quite right too; the more practice you get in this the better. A good lecturer will generally encourage you to develop the skills involved in *researching* a topic.

Reading is such an essential part of university life that you sometimes hear students say, for example: 'I'm at university, reading history'. You may notice this on the UK television programme *University Challenge*, for example, though they do not all say this nowadays. *Reader* is a title for a very senior lecturer (see Glossary).

Many new students have no concerns about reading, as the physical act of reading is not a problem to them. They don't really see reading as an issue. However, even these students can soon get bogged down in the sheer quantity of reading that seems to be expected of them. They often say that they need guidance on what is important.

For others, the physical act of reading can itself be a problem – particularly those with a visual impairment or *dyslexia*. Specialized software, tapes, and helpers reading aloud can help such problems to a certain extent, but again the students can be faced with having to deal with great quantities of reading. Less can be covered and it may be hard to work out what's important.

Students who are attempting to read in their second or third language can also be slowed down and feel that they cannot get through it all. There may also be cultural differences. In some cultures – and even some subject areas – anything that the lecturer tells you to read is important; in others, the lecturer recommends a lot of books but expects you to find what is important yourself.

Each set of students in the above three paragraphs has the same concern: to find out what is important. While some lecturers may give guidance on this, it is a question you should be asking *yourself* too. The forms in Figure 4.4 encourage you to set up a reading session with this in mind.

The next piece of reading...

Help yourself to prepare for note-making from a book. There are some questions you can ask yourself to help you to get the most from a reading session. They're only suggestions: if a less focused approach still works then that's OK!

Is this the right bit to read?
Before you settle down to intensive reading, you may have to do some other kinds. For example, you may have to:
- *remind yourself of your purpose;*
  e.g. are you looking for information, specific evidence of something, ideas about what is important, reinforcement of points made in a lecture, an alternative view?
- *get a feel for where the information is;*
  skim and scan a few books to gain an overview of the main themes, especially in relation to your purpose.

Once you're sure that this is the right bit of the book to read in depth, then answer the other questions below.

How long do I think it will take me to read this?
If you have a lot of reading, you may have to 'chunk' it into appropriate times. Don't be afraid of small chunks of time – e.g. 'I'll take 20 minutes and find out all I can about X.'

What do I want to find out from this part of the book?
Ask yourself a specific question before reading and then look for the answer. This makes the reading more interesting.

How is the information structured?
Get an idea of how the piece of text has been put together: are there subheadings? is there an overview or summary?
If the text is very dense, it can sometimes be useful to read the first sentence of each paragraph to get an overview of the main themes.

How will I have to use the information?
Do you need to make exact quotations? If so, ensure that you copy the words exactly, and put quotation marks round them in your notes so that you don't think that they are your own words.

Will you want to refer to authors' ideas? If so, it's a good idea to close the book and write down what you think the main ideas are in your own words. It is not advisable to take the writer's words and just change a few of them! You could change the sense by doing this, and also still be accused of *plagiarism*.

Figure 4.4 *continues*

Prompts for your next piece of reading

Question before reading	
Structure of text Subheadings (if any) Themes from summary/overview	
Answer to my question	
Other points discovered	
Useful quotation(s) Page number(s)	
Information for references/bibliography e.g. author, initial, date, title, page number, place published, publisher	

Figure 4.4 Reading prompts

University activities 5. Problem-solving

Some academic 'tribes' have always used problem-solving as a way of teaching their subjects to newcomers. The most technical parts of my engineering course were like that. I could trace my success throughout the course through an increasing independence in relation to problem-solving. At first, I just followed the procedure that the lecturer gave; by the end of the course I was able to talk about the procedures and even create my own problems (by asking myself how the water flow worked in my shower when I was washing my hair). Figure 4.5 shows some of the stages that I identified – they are relevant to subjects other than engineering too.

1 Follow set procedures.
2 Imitate lecturer, text, fellow students.
3 Recognize errors in my own work.
4 Compare practices with other students.
5 Recognize a specific procedure.
6 Identify the main principles involved.
7 Fill in gaps in knowledge.
8 Identify differences between different types of idea or object.
9 Give and receive feedback with other students.
10 Discuss abstract ideas.
11 Discuss my subject as a newcomer to the discipline.
12 Question and debate procedures.
13 Connect concrete and abstract ideas.
14 Find a way of expressing a problem in my own words.
15 Revisit topics and problems in a new context.
16 Create problems/situations relevant to my subject area.

Figure 4.5 Some stages experienced in developing as a student, with a particular emphasis on problem-solving

The first two of the stages in Figure 4.5, though necessary, will not be sufficient for a successful engineering student nor for other disciplines. Academic work goes well beyond following set procedures. However, that may be your starting point, particularly where there is a very precise procedure that has to be mastered, such as a mathematical equation.

Some problems do not lend themselves to set procedures, however. A relatively new approach to teaching – *problem-based learning (PBL)* – frequently uses real-life problems that are hard to define, and you are expected to work out what the appropriate questions are and find sources of information to help you to answer them. If you are used to following procedures – doing what you are told – then you may find yourself having to move into other actions in Figure 4.5 more quickly than you expected.

> I didn't like the PBL at first – we didn't seem to know what we were doing.
> And I couldn't see what it had to do with social work. Now at the end of
> the module our group worked so well that I don't want to split up and
> have to work with other people! I can see how it's relevant now, but I still
> think real social work will be much different.
> (first year student at the end of first semester)

The PBL approach is becoming increasingly common in professional areas such as medicine, nursing and social work. In the professions there are frequently some well-established set procedures – for example, handwashing, taking a blood sample, record-keeping – that must be learned and followed, and then some open-ended situations where there is no clear step-by-step approach that should be taken. By encouraging you to identify what you need to know about, instead of just telling you what you need to know, your lecturer is helping you to become an independent and critical thinker. At the same time, you will be working with other people and learning the value – and difficulties – of bringing several minds to bear on a problem. The lecturer's role here is to keep you safe and on track.

The range of PBL activities is broad, but the prompts in Figure 4.6 may help.

> What is the actual problem here? Are there several problems?
> Whose problem is it?
> Who else is affected?
> How did it arise?
> What is needed? What outcomes are required?
> What information do we have? What is missing?
> Where can information be found about this issue?
> How reliable are the sources of information?
> What are the barriers to solving the problem?
> Has this problem ever occurred before?
> What solutions were attempted? How successful were they?
> What would be the best way to present the findings? Are there any expectations about this?

Figure 4.6 Problem-based learning prompts

University activities 6. Placements

> I never thought that employers would be interested in the skills I'd developed in medieval history!
>
> (second year student, after a short work placement)

Usually, placements are associated with very vocational qualifications, where an element of work practice is an essential part of the degree: teacher education, nursing, social work, veterinary medicine are just some examples where a placement is essential. Increasingly, however, other students may also have opportunities to try out their developing skills and knowledge in placements. Like the history student above, you might find that your developing academic skills in sifting and analysing information might be very useful to a prospective employer.

Very often, as part of your placement, you are expected to keep a reflective journal. Even if this is not an explicit requirement, it is probably a good idea to do this. It can help you to write a good report at the end of your placement, and can also provide a useful record of any issues that are particularly interesting or causing concern during the placement. Figure 4.7 offers some prompts.

What is the main purpose of your placement?
Do you have to find the placement yourself, or will you get help?
Do you have any disability that the placement provider should know about?*
Do you know what you are expected to do before, during and after the placement?
Do you know what limits there are on your placement activities – what you are not allowed to do?
What are the health and safety regulations relating to your activity?
At the end... What have you learned as a result of your placement? How does it relate to the theories you have encountered in your classes?

* It is now illegal in the UK for a placement provider to discriminate against you on the grounds of your disability.

Figure 4.7 Placement prompts

Lecturers in context

Academic 'tribes' are complicated groupings of people. The following is a short guideline to some of the people you might meet: there is more information in the Glossary at the end of the book.

People in the department or division

The lecturer is not the only guide to your 'academic tribe'. You will hear a number of different titles (and sometimes even several titles for one person). For example, you may be expected to see someone with a title such as *personal tutor* or *counsellor* or *adviser of studies* fairly early on in the course to discuss your academic studies and to be a first point of contact. Sometimes this can even be a person who has nothing to do with your own subject.

There will be some people who are involved in teaching you who do not have the title lecturer. They might be *research* students – sometimes called *graduate teaching assistants* – who take on some teaching duties as well as their own studies. Research assistants are often employed on short contracts for specific pieces of research in a department, and they sometimes take on the teaching assistant role too. If you are doing a technical subject, you might have demonstrators working in your labs to show you specific procedures. *Technicians* are often very specialized and can be invaluable support for students.

Even lecturers have a variety of different titles. Some are *senior lecturers*, with promoted posts. An even higher grade is reader, a word that shows how important reading is for studying at university. In UK universities, the highest grade of academic staff is professor; in some other countries, the title is used in some form for all academic staff. A professor is sometimes said to have a *'chair'*, a term that originally referred to the piece of furniture where a professor sat to deliver a lecture. Professors use the title instead of Mr or Ms; you will also see the title *Dr*, which means that the person has a *PhD* (doctor of philosophy) or a similar qualification – a higher degree.

Most of your lecturers will not just be teaching; they will be doing research as well. So a lecturer might have many roles: teaching, research, counselling as well as various administrative duties.

There will also be administrative staff. You may meet people with the title administrator or departmental *secretary*, for instance. Often this is the person to whom you have to hand in a piece of coursework and who also knows a lot of information about the department and its staff (which is useful if you are looking for someone).

The wider context: people in the faculty or school

Most universities are split into *faculties* or *schools* – typically there are around four to seven such groups. So, for example, the subject behavioural psychology might be taught in a department of psychology in a faculty of social sciences. The faculty will be headed up by the *dean*, who is an academic who has taken on a leadership role within this particular grouping. This person might not have any knowledge of your own particular subjects. (He or she may not actually be a member of your own academic 'tribe'.)

Figure 4.8 shows how your academic tribe may fit into the university structure (but note that there are many variations on this). For definitions of the titles in bold, see the Glossary.

People outside the university

Your academic 'tribe' has a place in its own university, but it also has a place that goes across universities and beyond. This means that there are connections with:

- other universities;
- relevant professions, industry or business;
- the ideas of people who are interested in this subject across the world and through time.

Academics try to meet each other through conferences, where they give papers and have discussions. In a way, your own experiences of writing academic essays and participating in seminars are a form of initial training for such conferences.

You are likely to meet some other members of your academic tribe yourself – for example, when you have a visiting lecturer, go on a site visit or field trip, or engage in a placement. You should welcome any opportunities to broaden your understanding of your subject this way. Even if you don't meet these people in person, you should arrange to 'meet' them through their writing. By reading their books and papers, you are gaining vital 'tribal' knowledge.

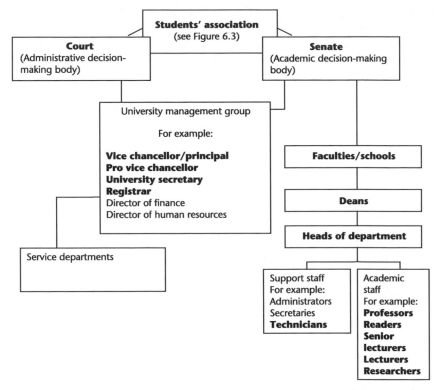

Figure 4.8 Organization chart for a university, showing the lecturer and 'tribe' in context

How to speak to your lecturers and tutors

There have been some hints throughout this chapter about what to say to university staff, but it is useful to spend a few moments thinking about your relationship to them. This is difficult because of the variety of people involved: some are very formal and others very informal. Many students find this confusing. If in doubt, it is probably better to be more formal until you get signals that you do not need to be.

However, in my own teaching I must confess to being very amused when students call me 'Miss' because of the practices they bring with them from school. At first when I heard this, I thought someone was hissing at me – I hadn't expected to be called 'Miss'. I usually explain to my students that I prefer to be called 'Christine' but if they are uncomfortable with this, they can call me 'Dr Sinclair'.

> That student I've just seen called me 'pal'. I put him right on that. I said: 'I'm not your pal – and don't you forget it.'
>
> (engineering lecturer)

If you regularly use words such as 'pal', 'love' or 'dear' in your day-to-day speech, you should be very careful not to use them with lecturers. Some (like myself) may find it amusing; others may feel that you are trying to patronize or be overfamiliar with them. In general, such forms of address will be regarded as inappropriate.

Don't assume that lecturers like you to use their first name; some prefer to maintain a distance by use of titles and surnames, and you may also find yourself addressed as 'Mr' or 'Ms'. These lecturers feel that the formality reinforces the lecturer's role as a person who is passing on the knowledge and culture of a particular community.

> I told the lecturer I didn't understand the lectures. When he asked what I didn't understand I said all of it! But he wasn't willing to help me.
>
> (first year student)

If you do have difficulty in understanding what the lecturer is talking about, it may be possible to discuss it after the lecture. But you have to help the lecturer to help you. If you say that you don't understand any of it, it is very difficult for the lecturer to know where to start. The lecturer may even conclude that you shouldn't be on the course, so it is not a wise thing to say anyway. It is much more helpful if you can frame a question that shows what you do understand, however little that is. Think about the following constructions and fill in appropriate endings to the sentence:

Is the main principle behind this lecture that . . .?
Am I right in thinking that the problem being discussed is . . .?
I think the key steps in the process are . . . Have I missed any out?
Is the metaphor/analogy here about . . .?
I understood that [word] means . . . Am I using the right definition?

Your own subject may require different types of question. The main point is that you should be showing the lecturer what you *do* understand so that it this can be corrected or supplemented with further information. You are much more likely to get help if you are prepared to make this kind of effort.

Conclusion

At university, you are introduced to the habits and practices of your academic tribe by a number of people, but particularly lecturers. While the lecturer is your guide to your new activities, most of the responsibility for becoming accepted into the tribe rests with you. This chapter has provided some prompts and questions for six different types of activity at university, where there are different things that you will have to do, with varying degrees of support from lecturers.

Whether you are in a lecture, a seminar, a lab, a library, a problem-based session or a work placement you should be asking yourself:

- What is the purpose of this particular activity?
- How does it relate to what I already know?
- What am I likely to have to do as a result of the activity?

These are not the only activities you are expected to engage in. There are more examples in the following two chapters.

Finally, you should remember that lecturers are your guides (and possibly gurus) in this new world, but much of what you learn will come from what you do yourself.

Note: This chapter has been emphasizing the lecturer in context. There are other people you will meet as a student, and some of these are considered in Chapter 6 when there is more emphasis on the *student* in context.

5 What do you have to do to be accepted round here?

So far, we've found out how the inhabitants of Planet University talk, how its academic tribes operate, and how lecturers can act as guides or gurus to help you find your way. At the same time, you've been encouraged to think about what you should be doing in response to what you find on the planet. If you want to stay here, you're going to have to do certain things in certain ways – particularly to say and write things in certain ways.

This is the chapter that deals with the language of rules and regulations relating to university life. It also encourages you to think about the kind of language you need to use to pass your university course: how you will show what you know through assignments and exams.

Universities are complex institutions with many regulations and also a lot of hidden 'ways of doing things'. Often students have told me that they have felt bewildered when they arrived because they just don't know what these regulations are – and what they are supposed to do. On Day 1, everyone else seems to know how to *matriculate* and where *registry* is (see the Glossary for both of these words). Later on in the course, when it comes to doing work that has to be assessed, if you don't know how the university works, then you might do some very good and very intensive work that proves to be unacceptable. For example, some students find that techniques they have used previously are regarded as plagiarism. What you say and write while you are at university will in turn contribute to what your university qualification says about you.

The chapter is divided into three broad sections:

getting in: the words you need to say and write to get into university and make sure you are officially a student there;
staying in: the words you need to say and write to stay in university: assignments, exams and other forms of assessment;
leaving: with a qualification – what your qualification says about you.

The second section is the largest and, as in the last chapter, there are some tips and prompts to help you with your studies.

Getting in

Despite my many years' experience of universities and college, when I applied to be a mechanical engineering student and was accepted, I more or less thought that was it. I forgot that I would have to go through a fairly lengthy procedure to be properly *enrolled* on the course. I possibly thought that because I was a part-time student it would be different, but of course I still had to make sure I was fully enrolled as a student on my course, a process sometimes also known as *matriculation*. This involved standing in various queues to tell people details about where I lived, what qualifications I had and how I was going to pay for the course.

If you are reading this before attempting to get into a university, it is important to recognize that there are a number of stages you will need to go through.

Use Figure 5.1 to see where you are in this process; further comments on the words in bold can be found in the Glossary. Even if you have already started your classes, it's worth checking this list to make sure you are properly in the system.

If you have never had any dealings with a university before, your local careers office or library will be able to help you with this list. A lot of information is available through the World Wide Web. International students find the Web particularly helpful.

Many UK universities can be easily found on the Web just by typing the name into a search engine. You'll notice that they have similar addresses, formed by the university name or abbreviation combined with .ac (short for 'academic'). For example:

Glasgow Caledonian University: http://www.gcal.ac.uk
University of Glasgow: http://www.gla.ac.uk
University of Paisley: http://www.paisley.ac.uk
University of Strathclyde: http://www.strath.ac.uk

A very useful site to help you to find individual universities in a particular area can be found on the University of Wolverhampton site: *http://www.scit.wlv.-ac.uk/ukinfo/uk.map.html*. As well as a map of UK universities and other higher education institutions, it also has some other helpful links for information before you start a course.

An essential website for prospective students for UK universities to visit is the one for the Universities and Colleges Admissions Service (*UCAS*). This is the 'one-stop shop' for all university and college admissions. Again, this uses ac.uk in its address which is: *http://www.ucas.ac.uk*.

Applications to UK universities are now made online through the UCAS site. Only in very exceptional circumstances will UCAS now accept paper applications. If you are not used to computers, you could go to your local library or find an Internet café, for example, and ask for help in getting on to the site. If you are at school or college you should be able to get help with the UCAS process from staff there.

The UCAS site offers guidance to people who want to know the benefits and costs of higher education, international students, parents, and people who are already in the system. It has information on deadlines, what to expect, frequently asked questions (FAQs) and opportunities to communicate with other people who might be attending your university and even doing your course. You can track the progress of your applications on the site too.

Figure 5.1 gives you a quick checklist on things you are going to have to do before you can enter the new planet. You might encounter several unfamiliar words during these stages – check the Glossary at the end of this book.

You will also need to find out about funding for your course, which is different in different parts of the UK and also for different groups of students; this is beyond the remit of this book, but see Glossary under *welfare*.

Much of Figure 5.1 relates to getting information and making sure you are in

Stage	What you have to do	Information sources
Select course	Choose subject(s) Choose mode of study (full-time, part-time etc.) Find institutions (universities and colleges) that offer this subject	University **prospectuses** and websites Careers advisers Local libraries University **open days** **UCAS** http://www.ucas.ac.uk
Select institution(s)	Choose where to apply	As above **Admissions officers** in the **institutions**
Be eligible to apply	Check qualifications Get qualifications if necessary	Admissions officers in the institutions
Apply	Fill in **UCAS form** online	UCAS
Attend interview (if required)	Prepare to say why you would be a good student	There may be guidelines from the institution
Accept offer	Accept offer in writing or online before closing date	UCAS/the institution itself
Enrol/ matriculate/ register	Attend institution at a specified time Show documents (e.g. exam certificates) Sign papers Be photographed Receive matriculation card(s) For some students or courses, other requirements e.g. a medical examination	Letter from the institution, received shortly before enrolment date
Attend induction	Attend session to find out about university, faculty or department	Letter from the institution Check institutional website too
Get information needed to start	Find out when and where your first classes are	Information given at enrolment. Check departmental noticeboards. Ask in departmental offices

Figure 5.1 Checklist for starting university

the right place at the right time and with the right documents. Often the language you have to use yourself will simply be signing your name – probably several times. But you will also have to say things about yourself – for example, in the personal statement on the UCAS form.

For some courses, you can expect to be interviewed before being accepted. This is particularly true of very popular courses where there is a limit on the number of students that can be taken on. Interviews are also often necessary for certain types of vocational course to ensure that you are the right sort of person for the profession. If you are asked for an interview, you will need to be able to demonstrate that you have the appropriate skills and attitude or will be able to develop them.

For all prospective students, it is a good idea to take stock of your own qualities before you start university. Most university courses now incorporate some kind of *personal development planning* (*PDP*) process where students are encouraged to think about the skills that they already have and those that they need to develop. You will have a headstart if you think about the issues in Figure 5.2 before you go to university, and it will also be good preparation for any interview.

If you are going to a different country to study, you may also have to demonstrate your ability to speak a language at a particular level. Most UK universities have staff who specifically work with international students and will tell you about any certificates you will need. They will also advise you about other necessary documents such as visas.

It is useful to ask yourself about your own skills and qualities before going to university as it may help you to decide which courses you should not apply for as well as those that would be a good option.

> Anyone who wants to do our course must have manual dexterity – be good with their hands. Though we tell prospective students about this, we do sometimes get students who really don't have it. It causes a lot of problems; it's almost impossible for them to get through the course.
>
> (admissions officer for a professional course)

Staying in: getting good marks

So much time at university is spent listening and reading that students sometimes forget that they will have to speak and write themselves. This is the section of the book that is most concerned with the words that you will have to say and write as a student. These words will be assessed in a variety of ways. Assessment methods are very much regulated by the university, which is why they are included in this chapter.

> I wish it was just exams! I don't see why I should have to do all this writing.
>
> (engineering student)

1 Why do you want to go to university?

2 What personal qualities do you have that will help you to succeed at university?

3 What qualities do you think a graduate in your subject area(s) possesses?

4 Which of the following skills are you already good at and which will you need to work at to succeed in your course?

   • Written communication
   • Oral communication
   • Working with numbers
   • Finding sources of information
   • Using statistics
   • Practical skills
   • Managing time and tasks
   • Other (what?)

5 Describe a project or task that you think you did very well.

6 Ask yourself a question like the above that might come up at an interview or during your time at university – and try to answer it.

Figure 5.2 Prompts for supporting statement, interview or personal plan

> I'm OK with essays, but my exam marks always bring me down. They're just memory tests – I don't think they're very fair.
>
> (social sciences student)

> If I'd known I'd have to do a presentation, I wouldn't have taken the course.
>
> (arts student)

Whatever you think about the assessment methods used at your university and in your subject, you probably have little control over them or opportunity to avoid them. Some people do deliberately choose their university courses on the basis of how they assess students. These students have read prospectuses and course descriptions very carefully, and have possibly discussed the assessment with admissions officers before coming to university. This can be particularly important for some disabled students, or students who have a strong antipathy to a particular form of assessment (for example, making a presentation). Once you are in the system, you probably have to accept that you will be assessed in a particular way whether you like it or not. (Disabled students, of course, cannot be discriminated against on the grounds of their disability and this does lead to some flexibility in assessment; nevertheless, you will still not have complete control over it.) When it comes to assessment, it's better to concentrate on what you can control.

I've realized that it's not so much how clever you are; you just have to be organized and be prepared to put the time in.

(engineering student, at the end of first year)

In this section, we look at the language of assignments, exams and other forms of assessment. The emphasis is on what you are expected to do and how you might write and speak in response to these expectations. You need to show that you know how to use the language of your new 'planet' and its tribes.

University activities 7. Written assignments

You'll find an example of a short essay in Figure 5.3 and of a short report in Figure 5.4.

My first essay was a disaster. I'd no idea how long it should be. I didn't know how to use the books. I just didn't know what they wanted.

(philosophy graduate)

They said I hadn't structured it properly. What does that mean?

(first year student)

We don't give out model essays. The students would just plagiarize them.

(lecturer)

I looked at a model essay and that put me off. I thought: 'I'll never be able to write like that.'

(first year student)

A professional writer would not submit a story or an article without researching other types of story or article valued by the publisher or other readership. But it often seems that students have to be treated differently. Staff do not like to show them other students' essays or model answers because they fear that they might just copy them, and some students do find model essays intimidating.

Of course it's not giving away any secrets to tell you that there are many university essays available on the World Wide Web. The sites that offer them (or offer to sell them) claim that their essays are for reference only and should not be submitted as your own work. If you use them just to let you know what an essay looks like, you will not be doing anything wrong. If you copy any of them out and present them as your own, you are guilty of plagiarism and there are severe penalties for this, possibly including being *suspended* from university.

It is hard to know how to write a good university essay when you have never seen one and don't know what lecturers are looking for. Essay writing that worked well at school or college might not be adequate now. So, I personally

Introductory comments on the topic	Student literacy is frequently seen as a problem in both schools and universities – by staff, by employers and by the media. There are several ways of describing this problem and, as they suggest different solutions, the teaching of literacy is a controversial area in both types of institution. The relationships between school and university teaching of literacy are particularly interesting: many lecturers believe that literacy is the responsibility of schools and that schools have failed badly. This essay argues that lecturers themselves have a role to
This sentence incorporates the essay question	play in helping students to achieve appropriate literacy, but their task needs to take into account the influence of previous experience. It explores the concepts that underlie this view and that might help lecturers to understand the teaching and learning of literacy.

How the problem is described	To begin the analysis, it will be useful to tease out some of the contested ways of describing the problem. Different lecturers and teachers are likely to be influenced (without being necessarily aware of it) by different ideologies such as those suggested by the positions described in MacLaren's (1988) framework:

(a) *Functional literacy:* This approach emphasizes the need for people to be able to perform particular tasks and is often related to employment. Literacy relates to skills and competence in reading, writing and speaking. Problems are described in terms of deficiency in the student, for example: 'Students can't write in sentences any more.'

Someone else's framework – described in my own words	(b) *Cultural literacy:* In this approach, the context of literacy is acknowledged, in particular the meanings and values associated with particular cultures. Problems might be described in terms of a canon: 'How can we ensure that students are familiar with the works of Shakespeare?' or, in the more liberal approach, in terms of acknowledging the different backgrounds and cultures that might be found in a group of students.

(c) *Critical literacy:* Writers taking this perspective emphasize the use of language in power structures, and see the problems in terms of students' relationships with the dominant power. Literacy is concerned with the empowerment of people – giving them a voice.

How I am going to use these definitions	How students read, write and speak is likely to be judged in very different ways, depending on the perspective of the staff member. It will be difficult to solve the literacy problem if staff cannot agree on what it is. The analysis below shows the different interpretations suggested by MacLaren's framework and the relevance of the associated concepts in examples both from the literature and from personal experience. It focuses on the students' perspective: their previous literacy practices, the rituals and procedures they see in the classroom, their relationship with the new language practices they encounter.

The problems faced by a new student are well-summarized in the statement: 'It's as if all the ways I've used before don't seem to matter here' (Lea, 1994). Lea's paper focuses on a group of undergraduates who had chosen to attend a 'Writing and Language Centre'. Many of them were mature students from non-traditional backgrounds and for some Standard English was not their primary dialect. Though Lea's student thinks her 'ways' don't count, they inevitably will affect her writing and her understanding of other people's writing:

Figure 5.3 *continues*

gaining access [to literacy events] can... be a matter of cross-cultural interaction between school culture and students' home culture.

(Bloome, 1994:102)

When students come to university, they are bringing school, home, social and possibly work cultures with them. If none of these seem to count in this new environment, then the student will inevitably feel alienated.

Summary of some writers who disagree with the functional approach

The functional approach might seem to provide the answer to this alienation: using Standard English as a medium of communication which all groups can access. Lea argues that far from being the answer, this is part of the problem. By focusing on language structure and form and not taking into account both the students' previous experience and the requirements of specific academic discourse, lecturers give students inappropriate and useless feedback. In this, she is agreeing with Fairclough that the lack of homogeneity cannot be 'fixed' by 'legitimized and naturalized orders of language being presented as legitimate and natural' (Fairclough, 1989).

After drawing out the implications I can introduce an example of my own

Fairclough believes that an emphasis on standards leads to an instrumental approach, especially when it is put in terms of the language tasks that students have to complete. Giving students tasks to do is more akin to training them to perform than educating them to be aware of language practices.

Research by Edwards and Mercer (1987) and Bloome (1994) suggests that students readily go along with an instrumental approach. Both of these papers describe what is happening in schools in a way which resonates with the problems experienced by first year higher education students. Edwards and Mercer investigate the role of discourse in classroom practices, finding an unanticipated emphasis on control in the school classroom. They conclude that students are unable to take control over their own learning: they end up depending on rituals and procedures, expecting and receiving cues towards these. The following example, taken from an observation during a higher education class, illustrates the same conclusion...

- Example of procedure – following from my own experience.
- A section on students' perceptions of the role of the lecturer.
- A comment on the deficiencies of a functional approach.
- A section on what the literature says about introducing students to particular ways of talking that they must adopt. This includes more examples from my own experience. There is also a criticism of this approach from the literature.
- A section suggesting the value of introducing the critical perspective – introducing the ideas of 'critical language awareness'

My conclusion summarizes my main points and shows how I've answered the question

... In higher education, an increase in numbers of students means that a wider range of cultural backgrounds have to be taken into account. Instrumental practices, begun at school and reinforced by social inequalities, will continue to interfere with learning until students can participate authentically in the academic discourse – and this goes beyond just learning to parrot its genres. It may be necessary to encourage critical language awareness not only for students but also for new lecturers. The broad concepts of functional,

Figure 5.3 *continues*

that lead to the literacy 'problem'. It is important that schools and universities do not adopt an over-simplistic view on what is required to solve the problem.

References

Bloome, D. (1994). Reading as a Social Process in Graddol *et al.* (eds) *Researching Language and Literacy in Social Context*. Milton Keynes, Multilingual Matters Ltd/Open University.

Edwards, D. and Mercer, N. (1987). *Common Knowledge*. London, Methuen.

Fairclough, N. (1989). *Language and Power*. London and New York, Longman.

Lea, M. (1994). I thought I Could Write Until I Came Here in G. Gibbs *Improving Student Learning: theory and practice*. Oxford, Oxford Centre for Staff Development.

MacLaren, P. (1988). Culture or Canon? Critical pedagogy and the politics of literacy. *Harvard Educational Review*, 58 (2).

Figure 5.3 Sample essay: literacy – from school to higher education

see no harm in letting students see some essays, ideally those that got good marks.

Some other lecturers agree with me and you may well be shown some samples in your own subject area. In Figure 5.3 you will see extracts from a sample essay written on the topic 'Literacy – from school to higher education'. I use this essay to draw attention to some general points about essay writing that apply to all subjects – so don't be put off by some of the language that probably does not relate to your own academic 'tribe'. Similarly, in Figure 5.4 I have included extracts from a report I wrote about quality management for my recent engineering course.

In this section, then, we look at what you are expected to say and write – and then think about how to go about that process. Remember that anything you say or write can be said or written in another way; the aim here is to help you to choose a way that is effective for your purposes. In Figure 5.8 there is a set of prompts to get you started.

Question 9

What do you think lecturers are looking for in an essay?

Study skills books, fellow lecturers and personal experience all suggest to me that there are four things you need to do to get a good mark in an essay:

The summary is the report in miniature. It often comes after the title page

Summary

The report considers the role for quality assurance during the design cycle of a compact electrical power supply unit. Quality assurance is crucial throughout all the stages of a design cycle. The contract should be reviewed during each stage to ensure that the customer's requirements are met, and associated documents must be carefully controlled. The reports highlights a minor problem that was addressed early on (compatibility with the overseas market) and a major one that prompted an overall review of procedures (the need to use a more appropriate material). The latter issue highlighted the need to consider company procedures, particular in relation to national and international standards. The company is now seeking certification under ISO9000.

A Failure Mode and Effects Analysis early in the design stage confirmed the necessity for lighter-weight material. A subsequent discovery of alternative material led to a change of design, but by that stage procedures and documentation were well established and the change was effected smoothly.

Contents

Contents list should be on a separate page. Page numbers are in a column on the right. Only include the first page number for each section

Level 1 heading

1. Introduction

Level 2 heading

Terms of Reference

This report has been commissioned by the General Manager of HAL computers to explain the need for quality assurance during the contract review and design cycle. The context for the report is that problems have arisen during this phase for the new compact electrical power supply unit for the current PC.

Outline Method

Quality assurance differs from quality inspection by 'building quality into the product in the first place' (Deming, 1986). This means that the design phase of a new product or component is critical. The design must meet the requirements of the customer and it must also be possible to implement the design at an appropriate cost. Key procedures for quality assurance relating to his requirement are:

- contract review
- document control.

Problems described in this report were particularly considered in relation to ISO9000, the international quality assurance standard.

Figure 5.4 *continues*

Level 3 heading ──┐ ── *Contract review*

According to ISO9000, the contract should be reviewed to check that the customer has stated what is wanted, that any differences between the original tender and the actual contract are resolved and that the order can be fulfilled. This will mean consider, for example: materials, methods, specifications, installation, service and disposal. ...

── *Document control...*

6. Design Changes

Eventually, a design must be ready for release – to complete one cycle of the process in Figure 1. Because standardization has been practised and design reviews and FMEAs have been undertaken, there should in theory be little need for change. Quality should be in the design, not in the subsequent inspection. However, in practice, it is recognized that changes are usually necessary to ensure the specification is met. Problems may not have been anticipated – e.g. discontinued parts – but as well as this, there may be potential advantages that have not been anticipated, such as new materials on the market.

According to X (1999), there are six determinants of Engineering change. These are shown in the diagram below, based on X's list.

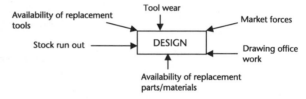

Number and label your figures ── **Figure 2: Design change control**

In the case of the power supply unit, successful fields trials suggested that the lightweight material proposed would justify the slightly increased cost of the final product. However, a glut of alternative material became available on the market shortly before production and future supplies of this material looked more assured that the one planned. Consideration was also given to the effects this would have on the tools to be used...

Conclusion

The difficulties faced during the design phase of this component have illustrated how the adoption of ISO9000 procedures is likely to prove of long-term benefit to HAL computers. A number of modifications have been made without even too much difficulty and even a change of design could be successful accommodated. Now that the systems and recovering procedures are in place, future designs should be subject to continuous improvement.

References

Deming, W.E. (1986). *Out of the Crisis*. Cambridge, MA, MIT/CAES.

X [lecturer's name] (1999). *Quality and Design*. Lecture Notes for Mechanical Engineering Z College.

Figure 5.4 Sample report: quality assurance during contract review and design cycle (based on a case study)

1 answer the question;
2 show evidence of relevant reading;
3 have a good line of reasoning (argument);
4 present the essay well, following academic conventions.

See especially Clanchy and Ballard (1997). A similar list has already been seen in Chapter 2 with respect to what universities look for in how academics and scholars express their ideas. Let's look at the how the essay in Figure 5.3 meets these criteria.

Essay requirement 1. Does it answer the question?

The essay question is: What concepts help educational practitioners to understand the teaching and learning of literacy? Figure 5.5 shows a way of analysing questions: ensuring that you take notice of words that provide the focus, scope or instructions for the essay.

Topic	Literacy
Focus words	Concepts, understanding, teaching and learning, help, educational practitioners (lecturers/teachers)
Instruction	What concepts? How do they help? Why are they important?

Figure 5.5 Breaking down an essay question

The broad *topic* of our essay example is literacy, but it is important not to just write down everything that is known about literacy.

The question *focuses* on concepts, understanding (and especially the educational practitioners' understanding) and both teaching and learning. A particularly important word is 'help' – it is necessary to say something about concepts that help understanding.

The *instruction* in the question is not explicit: the student is expected to identify appropriate concepts and say why they are appropriate and particularly how they help practitioners' understanding. See Figure 5.6 for some typical instruction words.

Notice how at the beginning of the essay I explain how I am going to answer the question. I indicate that I am going to take a stance relating to students' previous experience of literacy and show how the concepts underlying this view could help understanding. Later, after I've explored some definitions of literacy, I indicate how I will use these definitions in relation to examples. At the end of the essay, I again refer back to the question.

There are many other possible examples: a good dictionary may help you and there are similar lists to this on the World Wide Web (try searching for 'essay instruction terms').

Essay requirement 2. Does it show evidence of reading?

The evidence of reading can be seen in the *citations* (see Glossary) I have used. These are not only direct quotes, although there are a couple of those. I have

NB: The focus words might sometimes change these meanings, so just use them as a rough guide. An instruction that tells you what to do is usually a verb; sometimes, however, a noun or adjective might be involved. (I discuss these grammatical terms in Figure 5.14.) I have not included adjectival forms you are unlikely to meet in essay instructions. Sometimes, as in the example we're currently considering, the instruction is 'hidden' and you have to work out what it is.

Verb	What you are expected to do	Noun	Adjective
Analyse	Break down a topic/situation into its component parts. Say how these parts fit together, which is most important, what the main influences are	Analysis	Analytic
Compare	Find points of similarity as well as difference. You should be writing about two or more things. Say whether they are more alike than different. Can the features of one always be attributed to the other?	Comparison	Comparative
Contrast	Find points of difference. You should be writing about two or more things. Make sure you emphasize the differences between them	Contrast	Contrasting
Criticize	Analyse and pass judgement on. Make a specific examination, explore evidence and its implications before you make this judgement	Criticism	Critical (this is often combined with one of the nouns, meaning you must think about judgement)
Discuss	Identify the main points and look for evidence to support or refute any claims made. You may be expected to consider advantages and disadvantages, or the merits of a particular approach. It may involve an investigation. (This is a very popular word with lecturers!)	Discussion	
Evaluate	Provide an opinion or judgement on something, based on evidence. State the points for or against. Suggest the value of something	Evaluation	Evaluative
Explain	Give reasons for a situation, saying what is going on and why	Explanation	Explanatory
Justify	Provide good reasons and evidence for your conclusions about a situation; show that something is correct	Justification	Justifiable

Figure 5.6 *continues*

Outline	Summarize the main points or important ideas; give a general picture, without details	Outline	Outline
Synthesize	Build up, put together, combine (opposite of analyse)	Synthesis	Synthetic (rare in essay topics)
To what extent...?	Or how far...? You are expected to make a case but indicate its limitations or contradictions (This is quite a popular construction in essay topics)		

Figure 5.6 Meanings of essay instructions

also acknowledged people's ideas; these people are important for the concepts and theories that I want to present. I began with one person's framework, but I did not draw all the concepts from MacLaren. I used other writers' work to highlight the issues – for example, the way Lea rejects the idea of the functional approach.

> I'm surrounded by books and notes – and now I don't know what to do.
> (student writing first essay)

The student who said that had phoned me to ask for help. I had a mental image of her trying to drag an essay out of the books, when really the essay had to be from her own head, though the books would provide evidence and other types of support. She had to read the books first before she could formulate her ideas, but the ideas were her own (even if they were very similar to those of some of the writers she had been reading). She had to work out what her answer to the question was and she then had to select from the books to support the important issues she was presenting.

There are several purposes for reading; here are three you will use in writing an essay:

1 read to find out what the topic is about;
2 read to find answers to your specific focused questions;
3 read to find evidence to back up your argument.

Essay requirement 3. What is the argument?

Some writers (for example Cottrell, 1999) prefer to talk about the 'line of reasoning' rather than the argument. In the example essay, I am saying that a functional approach to literacy is an inadequate concept because it does not help students. I provide reasons for considering the other two approaches, and also reasons for finding problems with them. Notice some of the expressions I use to show where I am in the argument:

- This essay argues . . .
- . . . it will be useful to tease out . . .
- The analysis below shows . . .
- It focuses on the students' perspective: their previous literacy practices, the rituals and procedures they see in the classroom, their relationship with the new language practices they encounter.

The last one illustrates a particularly useful approach, especially near the beginning of an essay. Summarize what you are going to do (here I've listed three subtopics) – and then make sure that you do it!

When a lecturer is looking for 'good structure', this means a clear line of reasoning along with some signposts to show where you are. Figure 5.7 offers some suggestions for words and expressions that might help with this if you are stuck.

Essay requirement 4. How is the essay presented?

There are no spelling or grammar errors in the sample essay in Figure 5.3 (I hope). It is written in neutral language. It uses the appropriate conventions for *referencing*. There has not been space to show this, but it also has a separate title page, with the title: *Students and Literacy*, my name and the date. There are only two pages here, but for a 'real' essay, I would have set my wordprocessor to one and a half spacing, which would have used more space, and I would have

These will all need to be completed and adapted for your own context. There are many possible alternative words to consider; take your cue from the question you have been asked.

Phrase	Some alternative words to the highlighted ones (not synonyms[1])
The problem **explored** in this essay is...	identified, summarized, analysed, outlined, discussed
After the description, there is a section that **explains**...	suggests, offers, adds to, comments on, questions, puts forward, develops, focuses on, defines
The essay **concludes** with a...	begins, continues, expands
The main **issue** is...	problem, subject, topic, theme, concern, dilemma
An alternative **explanation** might be ...	suggestion, method, account, theme, sequence, structure, idea
Before any suggestions can be offered, it will be **necessary** to...	useful, helpful, advisable, appropriate, sensible, essential
The first principle **identified** in the literature...	suggested by, offered by, highlighted in, gathered from, acknowledged by, recognized in, established in
There is **good** evidence for...	some, significant, questionable, little, insufficient, contested, substantial, incomplete, powerful, adequate, appropriate, considerable
The **analysis** has shown that...	comparison, review, approach, evidence, report
Despite the evidence offered here...	because of, without, although, through, with the help of, against, in favour of, supporting
There are still some **concerns** about...	issues, questions, observations, doubts, problems, difficulties

[1] Synonym = word having the same meaning as another one

Figure 5.7 Some useful expressions

numbered the pages. Notice that I have a space between paragraphs; this makes it easier to read.

One of the hardest things to get right at first is the referencing – citing other writers' work. Some departments are very strict about the style you should use; others don't mind as long as you are consistent. Until I got used to doing it, I kept an example in front of me – from the reference section in a textbook – so that I could copy the style. In the essay in Figure 5.3 there is a quotation from Bloome where I don't want to cite every single word and I use ellipses (. . .) to show that something is missing. I also added a comment in square brackets to explain what the author was saying [to literacy events].

There are many books on essay writing that tell you how to go about referencing. It is also important to find out the requirements for your department(s). Ask at the departmental offices whether there is a handout on referencing.

Question 10

How is a report different from an essay?

Reports are factual documents; in business or industry, they are usually commissioned by a particular person for a particular purpose. The purpose, the readership and the scope of the report are sometimes known as the 'terms of reference' and it can be useful to make this a heading or subheading in your report so you are stating clearly why it has been written. The purpose of the report should always be made clear at the beginning somewhere.

Reports are much more structured than essays. The information is organized under headings and subheadings. There is less evidence of an argument; a report is much more a gathering together of factual information. However, often a recommendation has to be made and this will require reasoning. Lab reports also may need to show reasoning, but again the main purpose is to record the facts and present them in a coherent way.

It is useful to think about the beginning, middle and end of a report.

Beginning: *title page*, including a title that makes the subject clear and the date that the report is handed in;
summary, if requested; this is sometimes called the executive summary. It is the whole report in miniature, as seen in the example in Figure 5.4;
contents page;
introduction; this should say something about the purpose;
method; this might be part of the introduction, but in some reports (e.g. a lab report) it is necessary to keep it separate. It says how you went about the study.

Middle: This is where you will have a number of headings that are directly relevant to the topic. They may include:
findings; this is where you write the results of any experiment or investigation.

End: *conclusion*; there should not be any surprises here – this should emerge naturally from your findings;

recommendation; if requested (sometimes just a couple of sentences in the conclusion);
references;
appendices; these should include relevant information that is not essential for the report itself, for example, if you have used a questionnaire to gather information, you could put a copy of it in an appendix.

University activities 8. Examinations

This section concentrates on writing *fluently* in an exam. Figure 5.9 shows a set of prompts I use for a discussion with students who have had exam problems. I try to get to the heart of what is preventing this fluent writing: to find out whether it is a problem on the day itself or during the revision period.

Sometimes, the problem relates to how a student prefers to work and whether that can be translated into work under exam conditions.

I'm OK when I've got lots of time. But I feel I can't do myself justice writing an essay in an hour.

(mature student)

I don't know why I couldn't write much in the exam. I talked to all my friends about all the topics for weeks beforehand.

(business student)

The mature student in the quotation above was happy to spend time researching a topic, but the task of writing an exam essay demands something additional. She needed a skill in summarizing ideas quickly; she needed to practise writing under exam conditions.

The business student was from China. She and her friends talked in Chinese all the time, but her exam was in English. If they had talked in English about business studies, then she would have had more phrases and ideas at her fingertips during the exam.

There are many books with excellent advice on taking exams and revising for them (for some examples, see the references and bibliography). The emphasis in this one is on the language you will encounter during the exam and the language you need to use to show what you know. It covers the same ground as some of the other study skills books, but its main theme is a language one: *you should aim to be fluent in interpreting questions and writing answers*.

I am trying here to build up a picture of what you will actually do in an exam (that is, usually, what you will write) so that you can spend your revision time setting yourself up to do this. I encourage students to create a positive picture of themselves doing well in the exam, and then work out the steps they need to take. Writing in an exam then becomes a familiar activity.

Some students, of course, will write more than others. In some exams, you

The next piece of writing

Use the following prompts to help you to think about your writing. If you can't answer any of them just now, think about what you will need to do to ensure that you can.

1 What format are you expected to use?

Essay ☐   Report ☐   Dissertation ☐   Short answer ☐   Other ☐

2 What is the question?

If there is enough space, write out the full question below.

3 What is the question looking for?

What is the broad topic?

How is the question focused – which words are important?

What is the instruction? (analyse, discuss, resolve etc. – this may be hidden)

4 What might the answer look like?

If someone just asked you this question now, what would you say?

5 What are you going to read as your starting point?

Remind yourself of your principal sources of information.

Books:

Journals:

Websites:

Lecture notes:

Other:

6 What questions do you want to answer?

When you have done some background reading, you will probably start to formulate some questions for more focused reading. If you have any at the moment, jot them down here. It helps make the reading more purposeful (and more interesting).

Figure 5.8 Prompts for writing

My last exam

If you did not do so well in your last exam, what changes can you make to what you do on the day or during the revision period? Use this checklist to work out where you could make improvements.

On the day of the exam

it would have been better if I had been able to:

arrive at the exam room at a reasonable time ☐
read the instructions properly ☐
allocate enough time for each question ☐
ignore other people ☐
analyse the questions properly ☐
organize answers to meet the key points ☐
write a useful introduction and conclusion to essays ☐
recall the information needed for the questions ☐
feel confident about all of the above ☐

During my revision

it would have been better if I had been able to:

divide up the revision time to cover each topic ☐
allocate enough time for each topic ☐
organize notes to cover each topic ☐
be aware of information from throughout the semester ☐
practise answering questions ☐
identify gaps in knowledge ☐
fill all the necessary gaps in knowledge ☐
prepare final notes in a memorable way ☐

Figure 5.9 Prompts for an exam discussion

may have to perform calculations, operate some equipment, an instrument or a computer, or draw or label a diagram – using the language of your academic 'tribe'. Even in such examples, it is useful to think about how you make yourself fluent in this form of communication. Students who have to use a scribe to write for them also have to remember that the resulting writing has to show what they know – there are different issues here, but it is still necessary to be fluent.

In multiple choice exams, all you have to do is tick a box – that is, agree with one or more of the options put in front of you. While it still tests you, this is a very different activity from writing what you know. If you find multiple choice difficult, it may be helpful to cover up the answer, think what you would write, and then look for the answer in the options. You need to do this quite quickly.

All of these examples have two things in common:

- you have a particular task to complete;
- there is a limited time available to do this.

Like all skills, completing an exam question in a limited time is one that can be practised. Here is a set of questions that might help you to do this. Find out as much about the exam as possible in advance:

1 When is the exam – day and time?
2 How long is the exam?
3 How many questions are there?
4 Are the questions of equal weighting?
5 Will there be special instructions? (e.g. Answer one from each section)
6 What form are the questions (essay, short answer, multiple choice etc.)?
7 What topics could the exam cover (from course notes, past papers etc.)?

From your answers to these questions, build up a picture of yourself on the day of the exam. Can you work out what you are likely to be doing throughout the time slot? Keep it positive, but include what you might do to bring yourself back on track if necessary. Figure 5.10 shows an example of this kind of thinking.

From Figure 5.10, we can see what this particular student needs fluency in:

- analysing a question;
- making a rough plan;
- bringing back ideas on the topic – and recovering from a 'blank';
- writing an introductory paragraph;
- writing on themes;
- writing a conclusion.

Ideally, the student should try to practise all of these during the revision period. This particular student might then go on to ask the following questions.

I have to answer three questions in three hours. I'm going to allocate roughly 55 minutes per question. I'll spend the first five minutes reading the paper and choosing my questions. I'll start with my favourite topic, spend five minutes analysing the question and roughly planning the answer. I'll bring back all the ideas on this topic that I've set up during my revision. Then I'll write an introductory paragraph showing how I'm going to answer the question. Then I'll write on each theme. At 2.55, I should be writing my conclusion.

At 3 pm, I'll be starting question 2, even if I haven't finished question 1. I'll spend 5 minutes analysing and planning, then move into my introductory paragraph. At 3.55, I should be finishing this question and can perhaps pause for a minute to clear my head.

Then I'll start question 3, by analysing and planning. I'll have a few minutes at the end to go back over any blanks, or just to keep going with my third question which will be my least favourite (at this stage, I'll do whatever I think will get more marks).

If my mind goes blank at any stage in this process, I'll sit back and use my 'recovery technique' to get back on track.

Figure 5.10 Positive thinking about an exam

1 How much time is available to work on these topics?
2 When are these times?
3 How many topics should be covered in detail?
4 What is already known about these topics?
5 Where are the most serious blanks in knowledge?
6 How should revision time be allocated across subjects and topics?
7 How and when can the following skills be practised/tested within a topic:

- analysing a question;
- making a rough plan;
- bringing back ideas on the topic – and recovering from a 'blank';
- writing an introductory paragraph;
- writing on themes;
- writing a conclusion.

Your own revision questions might be different (depending on the positive picture you built up of yourself doing the exam). Figure 5.11 shows an extract from this imagined student's diary/time planner. Rather than panicking about all the topics that have to be covered, the student has allocated a specific time for topics and tasks within those topics. Note that these tasks might not take up a whole day; the student may have other things to do on these days (such as attend lectures or write assignments).

One of the things the student aims to practise is recovering from a memory blank. The best way to do this might emerge during a practice run of a past paper. When I had a memory blank in an exam, I simply reminded myself that this is something that happens, that people recover from it and that I had done sufficient work to prepare for the exam. I then thought about the 'triggers' I had set up to make the material more memorable (in my case, using mindmaps – see Glossary). For some people, the trigger might be more of a sound, remembering a conversation or a tape. Others remember what they were doing when they were revising – perhaps sticking Post-it notes to a poster on the wall. Whatever your trigger is, it brings back the language you need to complete the task at the time when you need it.

For all students, being able to remember working through the writing or other process that they are now facing will be a great help in an exam.

Wk beg	Mon	Tue	Wed	Thu	Fri	W/E
3 April	Topic 3 Review past papers Organize notes	Topic 4 Read chap 4–5 Practise writing intros	Day off!	Topic 3 Practise analysing questions	Topic 5 Identify blanks Sort all notes	Set up memory joggers Try past paper

Figure 5.11 Extract from a time planner

The advice, then, can be summed up quite simply:

- find out what you are expected to do (e.g. write, calculate or draw) in an exam;
- see yourself doing this well;
- get the information and techniques that help you to do it;
- practise doing it.

You'll be glad that you did these things when the exam comes.

University activities 9. Projects

Your academic tribe likes to do certain things, for example they:

- find out about something;
- experiment with it;
- perhaps create or build something;
- draw conclusions;
- write about it.

The form this takes varies from tribe to tribe, but a lot of them do it and when they ask students to do it, they often call it a project.

When you are doing assignments and exams, you are answering particular questions or following specific instructions. With projects, you may have to identify your own questions, though you will still find that there are some instructions associated with the exercise. Some projects are still quite tightly defined; they are just longer assignments. Often, though, the problem with projects is that they can get too big and lose focus.

Because of the many different uses for projects in different tribes, the guidance here is quite general but encourages you to engage with what you know about your tribe already. What do they like to do and why do they do it? Figure 5.12 has some questions to help you to define and write up your project. Find any that are relevant to you and see if you can answer them.

University activities 10. Giving a presentation

> I said to myself: 'Do I have to go through this anxiety every time I give a lecture?' I then decided that the answer was yes, that's just the way I am. I'm always going to be nervous about public speaking. Funnily enough, since I've accepted that, it hasn't been so bad!
>
> (lecturer)

For some of us, having to stand up and make a presentation really does feel like being on another planet. The people who seemed like reasonable humans a few minutes ago suddenly turn into alien beings when you have to stand up

Are you investigating a particular problem?
Whose problem is it?
What causes the problem?
Where might the solutions be found?
What does the literature say about the problem?

Are you following up a *hypothesis*?
What do you think might be going on?
Why do you think this?
Does anyone else think this?
What evidence would support this?
Where would you find this evidence?
What evidence might contradict it?

Are you comparing two or more approaches?
What are you comparing?
What are the points of similarity?
What are the likely points of difference?
How will you go about making a judgement between them?
Has anyone else made similar judgements?

The process of project writing is often in two stages: a project proposal and then the final report. While the questions above may help you get started in defining your project, there are also some practical considerations that will need to be thought about in your proposal.

Practical issues
How long will the project take?
What stages need to be completed?
What will you be doing at each stage?
What equipment/resources/access will you need?
Are there any ethical or safety issues?
Do you have any special needs?

The structure of a written project is probably more similar to a report than an essay, allowing you to use headings and subheadings (but check your instructions).

Figure 5.12 Prompts for a project

in front of them. The room looks unfamiliar and time seems to move at a different speed.

To get rid of this mental image, I use the same positive thinking technique to get through a lecture or talk as I advise students to use in exams – I try to visualize myself doing it well. I picture the audience smiling and nodding and that helps me to think about what I need to say to ensure that that happens.

The keys to effective speaking are:

- have a clear message;
- think about your audience.

People who appear to be successful at speaking off the cuff usually have a very clear message and instinctively know how to put it across. They are thinking about the effect on their audience, not about their own shortcomings. Those of us who aren't so lucky have to spend some time thinking about how to get this message over, and work out what will make our audience happy. Many students (and unfortunately some staff) when they make their first presentations, don't even think about the effects on their audience! Use the checklist in Figure 5.13 to help you to ensure that you have properly prepared for your presentation.

If you are nervous about public speaking, check that you have done all these things. If you have, you should be properly prepared.

I know where the talk is going to be held. ☐
I have seen the room and can visualize myself in it. ☐
I know what equipment will be available for my presentation. ☐
I know when the time of my talk is. ☐
I know how long I have to speak for. ☐

I know what message I am trying to get across. ☐
I understand the type of talk my audience appreciates. ☐
I know the main themes of my talk. ☐
I have a good sentence to start my talk. ☐
I have a good conclusion for my talk. ☐

I have practised giving my talk. ☐
I know how long my talk takes to deliver. ☐
I can give my talk without reading it. ☐
I can (look as though I can) make eye contact. ☐

I have prepared my overheads/PowerPoint slides. ☐
I know what my cue is to start speaking. ☐
I know how to link my talk with other people in the team ☐
(if appropriate).

On the day

I have my overheads etc. with me. ☐
I know what my message is. ☐
I know what my main themes are. ☐
I know my beginning. ☐
I know my ending. ☐
I know I can do this. ☐

Figure 5:13 Prompts for a presentation

University activities 11. Reflection and planning

Many universities have now started a process called professional or personal development planning (PDP) – or a similar process that may have a number of other names. This is where you record your own progress and your ideas about skills and knowledge that you need to improve. Some students are expected to keep a reflective journal, others are asked to fill in a form. In some departments, this is done electronically, for example as part of a virtual learning environment (VLE – see Chapter 7 and Glossary). You might hear the expression 'e-portfolio', for example.

You were encouraged to think about some of the relevant issues, at the start of this chapter (Figure 5.2) when you were thinking about topics for a supporting statement or an interview to get into university.

One of the reasons for doing this is that it has become apparent that students acquire a number of skills and other qualities at university but are not able to recognize them or articulate them. By writing down your intentions and achievements you are starting the process of putting together a portfolio of evidence that will be useful for your future career.

In some professions, the process of professional development planning starts at university and continues right throughout the person's working life. More and more businesses and industries are using this approach. They have good reasons:

- reflecting on practice encourages continuous improvement;
- identifying *critical incidents* (see Glossary) allows employees to take appropriate steps next time such a situation arises;
- being able to articulate progress increases people's chances of being recognized and valued for their contributions – the 'right' people are given the right jobs for the right reasons.

This whole process can begin with you making some simple notes about the skills you have, those you want to develop and those you are developing through your course.

> We now expect graduates to be able to identify and articulate their own skills; if they can't, then they won't even get an interview with us.
>
> (employer, multinational company)

Questions to ask yourself include: Do your departments run anything that resembles the PDP process described here, and in Figure 5.1 and in the Glossary? Will your PDP be assessed?

Here are some typical comments students make about themselves when they are looking at their own personal development.

> I need to improve the way I manage my time and getting myself organized. For my last essay, I put everything off until the last minute then I wasted a lot of time looking for things. I now plan to keep a file of stuff just for the essay, so at least everything is together.
>
> (first year student)

> I think I've demonstrated my ability to work with other people quite well. The second time I chaired a meeting of our team I found I quite enjoyed it

because I could make sure that we all knew what we had to do (I think I must be a bit of a control freak!)

(third year student, in a project group)

I've got so far behind because I can't use Excel. I've got hold of a simple book on it and I'm just going to allocate the whole of next weekend to make sure I can do it.

(second year direct entry student)

I didn't like the idea of being assessed on skills that I think you've either got or you haven't got. But now I've discovered that I can make some improvements – my course gave me a new technique I can use. I still don't think it should be assessed but my thinking has moved on a bit.

(first year student on a 'personal development' module)

What might you be asked to do for your PDP? There is a huge range of responses: some departments do not even use the expression but may use phrases such as 'professional skills'. Typical assignments relating to PDP or similar approaches include:

- assessing yourself with respect to a range of skills;
- keeping a reflective journal;
- creating a portfolio of evidence.

Some useful questions to ask yourself are:

- What can I do?
- What evidence have I got?
- How can I present this so it makes sense to a reader?

Perhaps the most important one for assessment purposes is: what am I expected to do?

Responding to feedback

When you do an assignment, you will get some kind of feedback from the person who is marking it, even if it is only a mark. Ideally, they will also have added some comments and these should be useful to help you with your next assignment. Even if you have done well, it is a good idea to read the feedback to see if you can discover why you have done well and if there are any areas that can be improved.

Often students don't read these comments sufficiently thoroughly, especially if they are negative.

When I got my essay back last week, I felt gutted. I just couldn't look at it for two days. I thought I'd done quite well and I've actually failed it. I've completely lost confidence. I've never failed anything before. I just don't know what they want.

(first year social sciences student)

I hear this kind of statement frequently from students who are worried about their work. Often, the failure can later be seen as a good thing because it has forced the student to engage with the requirements of the course.

Before you can respond to feedback, you have to understand it. Often students will say to me that they don't know what 'structure' means or 'syntax'. Here are some comments that students might get in feedback. Definitions of the words in italics are in the Glossary: you might want to try saying what the comments mean before looking the word up.

- The style needs to be more *academic*.
- Your *analogy* here is very useful.
- Your *argument* is not clear.
- A *citation* is needed here.
- You have used the incorrect past *participle*.
- Please write in the third *person*.
- This is *plagiarism*.
- The *register* is inappropriate.
- This is a well-*researched* piece of work.
- There are too many *scare quotes* in this section.
- The essay is well-*structured* with good *signposting*.
- The *syntax* is rather odd in your conclusion.

If you're struggling with grammar and have never been taught it, you might not know the different parts of speech and some of them might come up in your feedback. Figure 5.14 provides a list of these.

It is understandable that people get hurt by feedback; they take it as a statement about themselves rather than about one (rather small) thing that they have done. Some lecturers can forget what it's like to be on the receiving end of feedback and they don't hold back (however, I have heard some students say that they like this: 'at least you know where you are with that lecturer').

You'll be called on to give feedback yourself during your time at university and it is useful to have some principles to go on, whether you're giving it out or are on the receiving end. Figure 5.15 gives you some principles to work with. You should particularly note the last one – it's quite hard to do, but will help you to respond appropriately.

If you have failed an assignment and have to rewrite it, you should take into account all the comments that have been made. One useful tip is to write a letter to the person who marked it, explaining how you have responded to each point that they have made. An example of this is shown in Figure 5.16.

If you make all the amendments suggested in the feedback it is very difficult

Part of speech	Description	Examples
Verb	Word showing action	be, do, have, learn, teach
Noun	Name of person, place, thing, idea	mother, Paris, table, existentialism
Pronoun	Word that stands for a noun	I, him, it, this, whose
Adjective	Word that describes - usually goes with a noun or a pronoun	attractive, dusty, gentle, red
Adverb	Word that modifies a very or adjective (often ends in -ly)	fully, gracefully, usually, very
Preposition	Word that indicates a relationship	for, through, to, up
Conjunction	Joining word	and, but, or, while
Interjection	Word expressing emotion which is unrelated to the rest of the sentence (usually not appropriate for academic writing)	alas, ha-ha, wowee

Figure 5.14 Parts of speech

to continue to fail you. Whether you actually give the marker the letter or not is up to you; some lecturers do find it very helpful if you do this. The approach helps to ensure that you do not miss anything out.

University regulations

We've now run through a number of things you are likely to have to do to allow you to stay on this new territory. These have included assignments, exams, projects, presentations and personal development planning. There may well be other types of assessment too.

Because universities are so highly regarded, there is a strong emphasis on standards. This brings a language all of its own, some of which is relevant to you as a student.

The work you have to do to stay in the system relates to your specific academic tribe but is regulated by the university (or other institution) itself. There are added complications: in some courses, another *professional body* (see Glossary) also regulates the type of work you have to do. This is particularly the case with respect to vocational courses such as those related to medicine or law (and many others). For all students, there are *external examiners* from other institutions who may check the work you do to ensure that you have been judged appropriately.

1 Comment on the action, not the person
A weak structure for an essay does not mean a weak person.

2 Say what is positive about the action as well as what is negative
You don't want them to stop doing the right things!

3 Only criticize something that can be changed
It is very frustrating to be criticized for something you can't help – like being told you're too tall!

4 Be precise
Don't make sweeping generalizations that cannot be acted on.

5 Offer suggestions to help the person to make the change
It should still be the person's own work, but some guidelines for what would make it work for you will be helpful.

6 Be prepared to receive feedback in return
For example, if what you are saying is ambiguous, it would be better if it could be clarified.

7 Treat all feedback you get as if it were positive
Even if you feel hurt or slighted, try to respond as though the feedback is helpful and meets the above principles.

Figure 5.15 Principles of constructive feedback

Dear *Marker's name*

I have now rewritten my essay and responded to all the points you have made as follows:

1 Incoherent organization
I have rewritten the introduction to explain the approach that I am taking and have highlighted three areas that I want to look at. This means that I have now deleted some material that was in the previous version that I now realize is irrelevant to the question.

2 Lack of evidence to support conclusions
I have added three new sections containing the evidence from the literature for each of my conclusions. I have attempted to build up the case for the conclusion rather than just stating it.

3 Poor sentence structure
I have had some advice about why my sentences were incomplete – I had not realized that words ending -ing could not be used as full verbs by themselves. I have checked this version over for incomplete sentences, by reading it aloud.

Etc.

Figure 5.16 A letter to the marker

Your university will have *regulations* that will be very lengthy documents, written in quite a formal style. Here are some of the main issues that are likely to affect you, highlighting some of the unfamiliar language you may need to know.

Most of your assessed work will be dependent on deadlines: essays are due in on a particular date, exams take place at a particular time. Unless there are special arrangements in place (as, for example, for some disabled students) then you should regard these times as final. It will certainly not be acceptable to say that you cannot attend an exam because you are on holiday that week, for example.

Inevitably, there can be problems because of illness or personal problems and there are regulations in place to deal with this. Each institution has its own regulations, but there will be some similarities. Whatever happens, you should get advice about the right thing to do – don't just make assumptions. You should get in touch with your personal tutor/counsellor or whatever the equivalent is if you are going to be away from the university for any length of time.

If you need more time to complete an assignment, you will have to request an *extension* (be warned: you might not get it). If you have missed an exam and have good reason for it, then you may be allowed to sit it again during the resit period as a *first diet* exam. If you fail the exam or do not have good reason for missing it, you may be allowed a *resit*. You should check all the italicized words given here on your own university's website (there is also further information in the Glossary). There you will also be able to find out how many attempts are possible at assignments or exams – you will not be allowed to keep trying for ever.

If someone is ill over an extended period of time and does not complete their degree as expected, some universities may award a degree with '*aegrotat*' in brackets after it. This is the Latin for 'he/she is ill'. It doesn't happen very often.

Most universities now have a clearly defined policy on plagiarism. This is an issue that causes much concern for staff and students. It happens often, sometimes by mistake and sometimes because students think they can get away with it. And some of them do, which is very annoying for other students.

Christine: I can tell that you wrote the second paragraph yourself, but you copied the first one from a book. You'll have to rewrite it in your own words.

Student: How did you know that?

Christine: There is a difference in style and the first one doesn't quite 'fit' what you are trying to say, even though it is written more formally.

Most staff can tell. There is also now software available to detect it and universities are using it. In Figure 5.17, you'll find my handout to help students to avoid plagiarism and another 'offence' known as '*collusion*'.

You could be accused of plagiarism if you:

- hand in (as your own) work that was written by someone else;
- copy out someone else's work and hand it in;
- copy out sections of someone else's work and include it in your own submitted work without acknowledging it;
- use someone else's work in any of the above ways with a few words changed.

That 'someone else' might be the writer of a textbook or an Internet site. It could be a fellow student, though you might then be accused of collusion.

You could be accused of collusion if:

- you and another student submit identical or almost identical work.

In this case, it is possible that both of you will be penalized – so be careful about handing over your writing to another student 'just to get an idea'.

Don't worry about collusion happening by accident. Even when writing on the same themes, people express themselves in very different ways. This can sometimes be hard to see when you are working very closely together. It's OK to discuss things – in fact it's a good idea – but when it comes to writing it, you should work separately unless it is a team project.

Why does it happen?

For the reader, in any of the above cases, the only thing they see is that someone is trying to pass off someone else's work as their own.

For the writer, there are a number of reasons why it can happen. Here are a few:

Reason for plagiarism/collusion	How to avoid
The student doesn't understand the work.	Find some other sources of information.
The student needs to do the work quickly.	Start working on your essay earlier.
The student wants to appear professional.	You'll learn this through original writing.
It seems the only way to write it.	Shut the book and write what you've read.
The student can't be bothered with the work.	Make sure you're on the right course.
Other?	

You won't be accused of plagiarism or collusion if you:

- use other people's ideas to build up your own information or argument;
- acknowledge the sources of any writing you have used;
- use this writing as evidence for *your own* points;
- make your own comments on the writer's points;
- use an appropriate approach to referencing, e.g. the Harvard Method;
- discuss your ideas with other students and/or check over each other's work BUT hand in very different pieces of work.

A possible approach to writing

1 Make sure you understand the question.
2 Jot down any thoughts on the question any time they occur to you.
3 Try to get the books, articles and electronic sources early. If they are not available, see if there is relevant information in other books. Check contents pages, indexes. Ask a librarian for help if this is difficult.

Figure 5.17 *continues*

4 Read quickly initially to get a feel for the main themes.
5 Ask yourself questions about these themes, then read to find answers.
6 Start planning/outlining your response to the assignment.
7 Think about the evidence in the books that supports your response.
8 Identify any counter-arguments to this response.
9 Write your response, drawing on evidence as you go.
10 If you are using exact words from a book, journal or internet site, put them in quotation marks and acknowledge the source (direct citation).
11 If you are using someone else's main ideas or themes, acknowledge these too, even if you are not using their exact words (indirect citation).

Example of direct citation

The best advice to students is: 'Develop confidence in your own words' (Cottrell, 1999:122). Students who rely too much on other people will not be successful.

Example of indirect citation

Avoiding plagiarism may be related to building up confidence (Cottrell, 1999). As a student's confidence in writing grows, the temptation to copy will decrease.

Reference

Cottrell, S. (1999). *The Study Skills Handbook*. Basingstoke, Macmillan Press Ltd.

Figure 5.17 How to avoid plagiarism

Leaving with a qualification

You've said and written the right things to get in, and then you've acclimatized to 'another planet' by saying and writing the right things while you're at university. All too soon, you'll be leaving, hopefully with a good qualification that tells the world something about the sort of person you are. Of course this is worth celebrating, though different people have different ways of making that celebration.

> It sounds daft now, but when people said to me: 'Are you going to graduation?' I didn't know what they were talking about. No one in my family had been to university – we didn't know that there was a celebration at the end. And I didn't go, which was a pity. My mum would have liked the ceremony.
>
> (graduate, now working in a university)

The graduation ceremony is a very formal acknowledgement of your achievement – one that many people enjoy celebrating with family and friends – but it is only part of the story. It's worth thinking a bit about the time when you'll be leaving university even before it happens. Some students report that they feel as if they have changed their identity by becoming a graduate, and this can result in a mixture of feelings.

So what does your degree actually say about you?

I'm proud of my degree. It tells people I meet that I'm a certain type of person – I'm reasonably intelligent, have some useful knowledge and skills and can apply these in a variety of circumstances.

(recent graduate)

A degree can also 'say' something positive about you to people you've known for some time.

My degree will show those teachers who said I'd never make anything of myself!

(student with dyslexia)

Unfortunately, I have heard several students make a comment like the above. The degree will represent proof to teachers, family or friends that they have underestimated the student in the past. 'I'll show you' can be a very powerful stimulant.

Your degree also says something about you to prospective employers.

A degree tells me that they can stay the course – it's not just that they're intelligent but they're persistent as well.

(employer in a small company)

At the time of writing, graduates are gaining higher salaries and suffering less unemployment than non-graduates, despite increasing numbers. So a degree is saying something positive to employers.

We expect graduates to be able to hit the ground running.

(representative of a large organization)

Reactions to graduates are not always positive though.

There was a discussion [with my fellow students who all worked in engineering companies] about graduates and how they sometimes get looked down on because of their degree and sometimes don't know as much as people who've been doing the job for years.

Also on qualifications in general – Andrew said 'There's a lot of snobbery in engineering.' A lot of people who are time-served look down on others.

(extract from Christine's journal)

The snobbery associated with degrees and other qualifications can take a variety of forms.

> And it's the middle-class kids who get the degrees, particularly from elite
> universities such as Oxford and Cambridge.
>
> (Peter Wilby, Guardian, 28 July 2005)

Wilby was pointing out that increased participation in higher education has simply meant that more jobs require degrees and that people from poorer families are still underrepresented in universities and good jobs. And there can be major differences in status between universities.

> We want the best, so of course I'm looking at graduates. But I'm also looking at which university they went to and whether they got a good degree.
>
> (personnel manager of a major company)

I heard this last comment some years ago when I worked at an ancient university, but I understand that for some careers the status of a university may still apply. It is worth consulting your university's careers service for further information about such attitudes and approaches in employers. While you may feel that there is some injustice in the way things work, you can add the information to your store of knowledge about the world and try to take appropriate steps to minimize its effects on your own life.

These comments indicate that your degree can say a great many things about you, some of which you may not be happy about. It can say something about: the sort of person you are, how clever and knowledgeable you are, what you can do, how persistent you are, who you know, where you fit into other people's categories. The fact that a certificate can 'say' so much is another indication of the complexity of language and how meanings are condensed and buried in things. There are so many meanings in that one piece of paper.

It is also important to remember that just as university seems alien to some students, so graduates can seem like different beings to non-graduates. You may need to find ways of dealing with negative responses. These ways will depend on your personality: some graduates make sure that they don't come across as superior; others will not allow themselves to be put down for being 'overeducated'; some don't care what other people think.

However, the overwhelming reaction to graduates is a positive one – they are highly valued in society, they earn more, they are less likely to be unemployed. A degree is still a very prized qualification.

What's most important in all this is what your degree will say to you. No one can ever take it away. As with some of the positive thinking techniques used in this chapter, a picture of yourself as a graduate is a useful one to conjure up. What will you look, sound and feel like when you have a degree? And what will you have to do to take you there? What will be different about you?

Conclusion

Three stages of participation in university life have been considered in this chapter: getting in, staying in and leaving. As you move through these phases, you will be changing as a person in what you say, write and do.

> I've been reading this way for over 30 years. Now you're trying to change me!
>
> (mature student)

Though the student quoted above was rather alarmed at the prospect, he was correct – university life will inevitably change you in some way, and I made no apology for supporting this process by opening his eyes to new ways of approaching a book.

The checklists and tips from this chapter to help you through these changes have a number of features in common. You will need to:

1 identify what has to be done;
2 consider the time available to do it and the best use of that time;
3 look for relevant information;
4 evaluate information that you find: e.g. is it based on evidence?
5 organize the information in an appropriate way for the task;
6 show your reasoning so that people can see what you know;
7 present your findings in the most appropriate style.

These seven principles should provide a useful approach to life and language on another planet. They should enable you to enjoy the exotic locations and interesting beings that you meet, even if you can't always understand what these people are saying. Use the checklists and the Glossary here to help you to interpret what you have to do to gain entry, stay in university and leave with a qualification.

In the next chapter, we look at some of your fellow travellers and how they can help you on the journey.

6   I thought I was the only one who felt like an alien

You are not alone

I often ask new students what they are most looking forward to and what they are most concerned about in coming to university. Over two decades, the responses have changed very little – though there is now more emphasis on financial worries than there used to be. Two particular responses come up over and over again though, and in answer to both questions. Students are looking forward to and worrying about the same things:

- coping with the workload;
- getting on with people.

I remember asking a large group of students to fill in a questionnaire and reporting to them a couple of days later that around 75 per cent of them had used the exact expression 'coping with the workload' in reply to the question 'what are you most concerned about?' The relief for some students was visible: it can be very reassuring to find out that other people have the same concerns.

We are social creatures; it matters to us what other people do and think. Even very independent people who don't want to 'follow the herd' are affected by what other people do. What others do can have both positive and negative effects; the actions of other people have a considerable influence on the context in which we perform our own actions (whether we like it or not).

This chapter looks at some of the social issues that might arise when you start at university. Like the rest of the book, it emphasizes language practices – what people say and do through language. Many of the pleasures and pitfalls of a new social life depend on things you say and how you say them. No one else can tell you exactly what to say (nor should they) but a little understanding of how language works in groups may help you to be more aware of how you want to respond in new situations.

The chapter is illustrated with a case study from the west of Scotland. This is fictional, but is based on my own experiences as a student and the experiences of the students who come to see me. My own journal has given me some insights into how students can work together (and sometimes how they have difficulties with this).

The chapter concludes with a section on the student in context – thinking about who represents and supports students, where you live and general issues about your well-being. Again, the focus is on language; for example, there is not much point in having sources of support if no one tells you what they are called! And it's amazing how many final year students have told me (at all three universities where I've worked): 'I've only just found out about your department's services.'

Case study – four students meet

Four students have arrived for their first class at the University of the West of Scotland. They are a little bit late as it was quite difficult to find the classroom. The lecturer has already begun to speak. There are four seats together near the front of the large lecture theatre and the students slip into them quietly. Here is some information about them.

Anne

Anne has just left school and comes from a small village on the east coast. She doesn't know the Glasgow area very well. She lives in student accommodation. She enjoyed *freshers'* week, but is keen to get on with the real work. She's a bit concerned that she will find it difficult and thinks this lecture will give her an idea of whether she can cope.

Khalid

Khalid was brought up in Glasgow and still lives with his parents, who are very proud that he has gone to university and will be quite strict with him to make sure he stays. This is because he didn't do particularly well at school and his parents blame his friends for that. He is 20 years old and spent a couple of years at college getting the qualifications he needed to enter university. Khalid wants to do well himself, and like Anne, is keen to get started.

Joe

Joe is wondering whether he should tell this lecturer about his dyslexia and ask for a copy of his overheads. His concern about how to handle this is occupying his mind and he finds it hard to concentrate on what the lecturer is actually saying. He's just turned 18 and thinks university life is going to be good. He has to travel an hour a day to get here, but the train service is not too bad. It was a little late this morning though.

Maria

Maria is a bit concerned at how quickly the lecturer will speak. Over the three days she has been in this country, she has found everyone she has met speaks very quickly and with a very strong accent. She has already studied this subject in her own country but she wonders if her English is going to be good enough. She is a little older than the others – 26.

The four students take out their notebooks and make notes on what the lecturer says the course will cover. The lecturer then proceeds to work through an example of a particular type of problem. The time passes quite quickly; here are the thoughts at the end of the class.

Anne:	That's OK – I managed to follow it all.
Khalid:	I wrote about the same amount of notes as other people.
Joe:	I will ask for overheads but I did understand it.
Maria:	I wonder if he'd let me tape his lectures to get the words I'm missing.

At this stage, the students are most concerned with their own performance in the lecture. If they are interested in other people, it's really to compare experiences. They chat to each other as they leave the lecture theatre and are relieved to discover they had all felt a bit apprehensive and embarrassed about being late.

The early days at university – freshers' week, induction programmes, getting registered – can all seem quite confusing, especially if you're late and feel you have missed something. This situation is described by Kevin Sampson, near the start of his novel *Freshers*. The narrator of the story, Kit Hannah, who has arrived late because he didn't like the idea of freshers' week, is approached by a welfare officer for his hall of residence:

> Now, tell me, who are you and why haven't I seen you yet? Did you come to Registration?
> Her intention is reassurance and inclusion. She alienates me immediately with yet more implications that I've Missed Out.
> (Sampson, 2003:14)

The mixed emotions that go through some students' minds when they land on their new planet are captured well by Sampson. Kit agonizes about meeting people, thinking it's already too late – then starts to feel it might not be so bad.

> No one here is a threat to me. It's going to be fine. I still don't feel as though I can just barge over, sidle into a group and, like, intro*duce* myself, but I know intuitively that if I do, when I do, it's all going to be OK.
> (Sampson, 2003:17)

Breaking the ice with other people is often easier when there is some shared experience to comment on: having to stand in yet another queue, difficulties in finding buildings, where you are in the matriculation process. What to say once you've made the first comment can be difficult, especially for shy people. Experience suggests that some ice-breakers are more successful than others (see Figure 6.1); however, students with a flair for humour or irony may well get away with the ones I'm suggesting don't work! (And don't worry if you've already used the less successful ones – you can probably laugh it off later. A lot of people do the A-levels one!)

In general, when you first meet people, it's best to avoid personal comments or questions that might be seen to be challenging them. As well as the queues

May work as an ice-breaker	Less successful openings
How long have you been standing in this queue?	I hate this place already and all these people
I come from xx. This is the first time I've been here	That's a weird accent you've got
I need a coffee. Do you know anywhere round here?	You look too old to be a student
This is such a change from school/college/work etc.	How many A-levels/highers have you got?
I like your jacket (or whatever)	Why are you wearing that?

Figure 6.1 Ice-breakers

etc. already mentioned, there are many old standbys that people in the UK talk about – weather, traffic, train delays, last night's TV. This kind of conversation seems pointless to some people, but it plays a very important function. It is known as 'phatic' communication (a term you'll only need to know if you're studying certain types of subject such as anthropology, so I haven't put it in the Glossary). Phatic communication is speech used for social reasons rather than anything else. It often communicates feelings rather than ideas – such as the expressions some people use when their team scores a goal.

Even the expressions that work better might not work with some people. Be prepared to accept that some students will be feeling very awkward and shy, some might be worrying about something, some may even have decided that you are not the type of person they want to talk to. The last reason is quite rare, but there can be gender or cultural issues behind it.

And if you do talk to someone that you quickly realize is going to be a person you'd prefer to avoid, remember that you are not obliged to be friendly with everyone. Some expressions that can be useful for getting rid of unwanted attention are:

• I don't think I'm going to be around much.
• I don't want to make too many arrangements at this point.
• I'm going to have some personal issues to deal with in the next few days.
• I've got a few commitments at the moment.

You don't have to say what these issues or commitments are – just say you want to keep them to yourself. This topic will be considered in more detail under the heading of 'Your decisions about belonging'.

Don't worry if you still haven't spoken to anyone by the end of the first week. It's a bewildering time, and all the exhortations to 'break the ice' and comments that 'you'll meet loads of new people' can seem hollow if you're feeling out of your depth, lonely or confused. It takes some people longer than others to get to know new people; I have heard of cases of people who didn't speak to anyone for a whole *semester* but eventually became very influential participants in the university. You'll find your own time for making contact.

Signs of belonging to a group

The case study continues, with some examples of evidence that the students are starting to form a group. In addition to that, they are starting to think about their own identities within this particular class of students.

Case study – a group is forming

Anne, Khalid, Joe and Maria find themselves sitting in the same seats for every lecture (most students in the class seem to go automatically to the same seats each time). Here's an extract from a conversation about five weeks into the course.

Anne:	I'm really finding this hard; I'm dreading the test next week.
Khalid:	What – you? Don't give me that. You get As. Finding this hard, indeed!
Anne:	One A. And that was a total surprise, especially when I was late for the test. Talking of late, where's Joe this morning?
Maria:	I've had a text from him; he's missed his train. He wants me to tell Dr Jones because he will need her overheads.
Khalid:	The 'laties' strike again. We're getting quite a reputation.
Anne:	Not you. You've been here on time every day except that first day. You're the only proper student among us.
Khalid:	A student! Oh no, don't say that. They're those people that sit for three hours in a pub with a half pint of soda water and lime.
Maria:	Not the ones in my hall of residence – they certainly hadn't been sticking to soft drinks last night.
Khalid:	All my mates keep teasing me about being a student. They ask how school's going. They don't even know I'm at uni. I just tell them I'm still at college.
Maria:	That's sad. You sound as if you're ashamed of being a student.
Khalid:	No, I think I'm just getting used to the idea, that's all. And it's nice to be one of the 'laties' rather than the

'swotties' over there. Or the backseaters who couldn't give a toss at the back.

[The lecturer comes in.]

Khalid: Hey, that's not Dr Jones.

Lecturer: Good morning. I'm John. Mary Jones is ill today so I'm taking this class. Now, can you tell me when you usually finish?

Khalid: We usually stop about half past.

Lecturer: Are you sure? The class is timetabled for two hours.

Several voices: Yes, half past.

Lecturer: Students always say that. Just like they always say we get two hours for lunch! Well, we'd better get started as there's a lot to get through.

[He writes an equation on the board.]

Khalid: How are we supposed to know this?

Lecturer: You're just going to have to accept it for just now.

Khalid: [muttering] I wish I was back at college. They explained everything there. Maybe my pals are right.

Maria: Just get it down. I did this last year – I'll talk to you about it later.

Khalid: Good – Joe'll need it too. I'll tell him you're our new teacher. And thanks.

Maria: OK. Shut up now and listen.

Once people start getting to know each other, they have more to talk about. Because these students have very different backgrounds, they may still find it necessary to be cautious, so that they avoid causing offence. However, it is now possible for Khalid to tease Anne about her A grade using a sort of mock derision that is common in the west of Scotland. Maria can feel comfortable about telling Khalid to shut up – she certainly wouldn't have done that a few weeks ago but Khalid's own bluntness makes it feel safe.

The group already has a shorthand word for themselves: the 'laties'. It's not a real word at all, but means something to all of them because of the number of times some of them have been late. If one of them had tried to apply this word to themselves on the first day, it probably wouldn't have worked – at that stage, they didn't have that kind of relationship.

Each student is developing an identity as a student, but the exchange shows that this is not straightforward. When the lecturer says, 'Students always say that', he is positioning them as a group. A lecturer said something similar to a group of us in my class; it gave me a strong sense of solidarity and I was happy to be regarded as a typical student, even if there was some criticism behind it. But not everyone is sure about accepting the identity of 'student' and there is a hint of that in Khalid's comments about his mates.

Sometimes, the issue of having more than one identity can lead to stark choices:

I told them that I didn't want to hang about the pubs and bookies any more; I actually liked spending my time reading poetry. For a working class guy that was unheard of. But I had to move on.

(graduate)

Khalid does not want to give up his non-university mates, and is finding ways of separating his identity with them from his identity as a student. In accepting an identity as a student, Khalid may have to adapt some ideas – and there is a suggestion that he expects the lecturer to explain things in a particular way, especially as he was used to that way at college. It won't necessarily be the same.

Here Khalid is benefiting from being part of a group; it is clear that they can support each other in trying to understand some of the university material. Mature students in particular are often very good at forming support groups; all students can potentially benefit from creating a study group. Such groups often evolve informally, and often, as in our case study, because of where people habitually sit in the classroom.

When I was an engineering student, we tended to sit in the same section of the room each week. We got to know the people around us. However, by the end of the first year, as it was a small class, we had probably all spoken to each other. When we started our second year, I recorded our reunion in my journal.

First night back – project night

Evidence of group support – pleased to see each other. John said: 'You should be sitting over here' – so that I'd make a grouping with himself, Andrew and George. He talked to me about projects. . . Simon and Ross were trying to work out the minimum they could do for their project. Sandy asked me about degrees [at the university where I worked] and whether he could fit it in with his job. I promised to find out. Peter told me his partner's doing a course at the same time and nodded quietly when I said: 'So everything's going well then.' [This was a reference back to an earlier conversation.] He's thinking of changing his job. Spoke to or nodded to most people.

(extract from Christine's journal)

People who have been in a small class at a school or college might recognize the kind of friendly greetings that happen after a summer break. I was conscious of feeling included, despite being the only woman in the class. By this stage, we had a lot of shared experience and previous conversations to refer back to. Some of these were about the course itself, but some had got on to other topics. All of this can be seen in the short extract above.

In this class, I was particularly friendly with the three men who sat at nearby desks. The discussion we had about projects was very helpful to me. We all offered each other ideas and helped each other when we were stuck. Here are a couple of examples I noted of a type of talk that people use when they are comfortable in each others' company.

Andrew, sitting next to me, heard me mutter about the bolt I was attempting to draw using the computer aided design (CAD) package:

Christine: What are the dimensions of this?
Andrew: Well, it's called an M20.

I had interpreted this label as a parts number and it never occurred to me that the '20' could represent a size. I would have been stuck with this for some time if it had not been for Andrew.

On the same day, I was in turn able to help John:

John: If you're computer illiterate and they say, 'press return', you
              say 'eh?'
Christine: It's the carriage return button – this one.

John had looked in vain for the button with 'return' written on it; the symbol for carriage return was so familiar to the person who wrote the instruction that it must have seemed 'obvious'.

This general chat, illustrated in the case study and in my own experiences, often seems so casual that we don't give it any thought. But it can make a huge difference to a student's progress. It was particularly important in this class; the lecturer was off sick for much of the module and the students did have to help each other. Those who were sitting next to the student who already had a lot of experience in CAD benefited the most.

> Andrew and I both felt we were making progress but we seemed a long way behind everyone else. Some people's progress was very dependent on where they were sitting – there was much peer support. Andrew likes this but is concerned about the blind leading the blind – though he has helped me a lot, e.g. there was an assumption in the title of a component about one of its dimensions – this was something I couldn't work out.
>
> (extract from Christine's journal)

Andrew's concerns proved to be well-founded: he and some other students were using the computer software in the wrong way, drawing something by eye instead of making calculations. Fortunately, a lecturer was available to correct this before they reinforced each others' ideas too strongly. So although the social group is useful, it is important to have experts around as well.

It is very easy to get into a state of 'group think'. Our whole class turned up in the wrong room at one stage, each reinforcing each others' ideas that this was the correct classroom for the new module. It had to be the right place if we were all there. But the lecturer was waiting for us in another room. Something is not necessarily right just because 'everyone says so'.

Your decisions about belonging

When students' socialization reaches the stage that they can help each other through apparently casual chat, it can be very comforting. But sometimes a student can find themselves in a group where they do not feel comfortable.

> I can't get used to the drinking culture in this country. The other people from my hall – I like them at the start of the evening, but by the end they really get on my nerves. They talk such rubbish. And they make themselves so ill! It can be unpleasant sometimes.
>
> (international student)

This student eventually stopped going out with this particular group of people, though she still often chatted to them in the communal kitchen. She joined a number of clubs where she met people she was more comfortable with.

The people you meet might be in the same hall, the same class or the same part of a lecture theatre – these conditions are not necessarily going to make you compatible. (It is amazing, however, how often lifelong friendships do start just because of a casual chat outside a lecture theatre.) In our case study, the relationships are beginning to build in a promising way, but Anne is beginning to wonder about some other people she is meeting.

Case study – choices

The class has been asked to get into groups of three for project work. This could be awkward for a group of four people who are just getting to know each other, and Anne thinks she has the solution when two people from her hall of residence suggest that she joins them. It seems particularly convenient as they can meet easily. But six weeks have passed and their 'meetings' have consisted of going to the union and meeting some other people (who irritate Anne). She's beginning to feel uncomfortable and confides in the others over a coffee after a lecture.

Anne: You all seem to be so well on with your project – we haven't even started.
Maria: You're too busy having fun!
Anne: I wouldn't call it fun exactly. Sitting for hours listening to loud sexist knowalls who think they're funny! And knowing that the

	chance to get a good mark's just slipping away. It's really beginning to get to me.
Joe:	Have you done any work at all?
Anne:	I've done some, but whenever I want to talk about it, Alan and Kate just tell me not to be so serious. They've invited me to a party in Edinburgh this weekend. It means staying the night and getting no work at all. The project's bad enough, but I'm more bothered about the party. Alan and Kate are OK but the thought of spending hours with their creepy friends just doesn't appeal.
Khalid:	Just tell them that. 'I'm not going to your party. You can't make me!'
Anne:	It's not so easy.
Khalid:	Anne – don't be such a wimp. Look, I'll tell them. I'll just say: 'Stop bothering our wee Annie if you know what's good for you – and do some work. And buy some better clothes while you're at it.'
Anne:	You would, too. Don't you dare say anything!
Maria:	What you need is some assertiveness training.
Joe:	Who needs it – Anne or Khalid?

Assertive language

> When I see first year students, they often look as though they could do with some assertiveness training. Their heads are down, shoulders drooping, no eye contact – if they just straightened up a bit they'd look more confident.
>
> (lecturer)

After speaking to the lecturer in the quotation above, I looked round the campus and saw what she meant. It's hard to use assertive language if your body is totally denying it. And the droopy body language can be mistaken for either side of the non-assertive spectrum – passive or aggressive. It says, 'I don't want to speak to you because':

(a) I'm scared of you (passive);
(b) I don't like you (aggressive).

Usually, neither of these is the impression you actually intend to give. So the first stage in using assertive language is to think about what your body is saying. It is possible to become more confident and more assertive simply by acting the part. (See the Bibliography for further reading on this topic.)

Someone like Anne in our case study who has some uncomfortable things to say to other people has to ask herself a number of questions:

1 What do I want to happen?
2 What (if anything) am I prepared to do in return?
3 What does the other person want to happen?
4 What am I willing to concede (to give up or to allow to happen)?
5 What am I not willing to concede?

Question 11

What do you think Anne's answers to the questions above might be?

See the comments in the Appendix and read the next stage of the case study to see how her answers helped her in the dialogue with Alan and Kate.

Joe's question about whether it was Anne or Khalid who needs the assertiveness training is a valid one. Khalid's proposed response would have been inappropriate (too aggressive) because Anne still has to work with these people on her project. This is why the questions to support an assertive response take the other person's needs into account. This is sometimes known as aiming for 'win–win' – both sides come out of the situation feeling OK.

Case study – moving on

Anne has decided that she does not want to socialize with Alan and Kate but wants to keep on good terms with them. Here is the conversation she has with them when she tries to tell them this.

Anne: I just wanted to let you know that I won't be coming to the party on Saturday. . .

Kate: Why not?

Anne: . . . but it would be good to meet on Sunday evening when you're back to talk about the project. By then, I'll have an outline of the things we need to be doing.

Alan: Oh come on Anne – we've loads of time for the project. Come to the party.

Anne: No, I'm not coming to the party. But I will do a bit of work before I see you on Sunday. And I'll have a huge pot of coffee waiting for you to get rid of the last bit of your hangover.

Kate: We'll need cake as well! But why aren't you coming?

Anne: I have things I need to do. I don't particularly want to go into it. So I won't be coming, but we will meet in here at 8 on Sunday, we'll have a coffee and we'll get started on the project. Just half an hour, that's all at this stage. You probably won't be fit for any more! I really want to make a start on this project.

Kate: What things do you need to do?

Anne: [firmly] Sunday, 8 o'clock. We'll talk then. I have to go now. Have a great time at the party. Don't do anything I wouldn't do.

Question 12

At the end of the encounter, Anne feels relieved. She has got what she wanted. What techniques did she use?

Informal and formal groups

In the case study, we have seen that people naturally form groups because they share common interests or just like each other. There are also groups that people have to be in; for example, because they are working together on a project.

Sometimes, in the naturally formed groups, some interesting things happen to language. People begin to speak the same way, using the same grammatical constructions, slang, words that they've made up (like 'laties' in the case study). Like taste in clothes and music, the way you speak signals to other people how you relate to particular social groups. It can also exclude you from other groups. This process tends to happen naturally; it is only mentioned here because it offers an explanation for why people start speaking differently with different groups and why it might be hard for you to be accepted by one group or another.

At university, there can be a clash between the social language of the particular group(s) you belong to and the 'educated' language of the academic tribe. So you might be trying to acquire the language skills of your particular subject area at the same time as adjusting your social language to the norms of a new group of friends. Some students say that they find this difficult – they start to wonder who they are.

> I seemed to speak in two different ways – a 'posh' way in tutorials and more sort of slangy at other times. I got teased about it sometimes. They said I sounded like Princess Anne when I was trying to impress the lecturers. But I didn't do it deliberately. And I worried that they thought I was a snob.
>
> (graduate)

Most people will experience some version of this; we all tend to speak differently with different groups of people, even though for some it might only be a slight difference. You probably speak differently to a parent or partner from the way you do to someone you've just met, for instance.

People don't always adapt their speech to their new group. For example, in the case study, English is Maria's second language. However, she knows the correct past participles of irregular verbs and is at first shocked when she hears Khalid say 'I've wrote about 500 words of my essay.' Eventually she realizes that this is local dialect, but she still wouldn't use this expression herself. As she gets to know Khalid better, she is able to suggest to him that he avoids this usage in essays and formal presentations (see Chapter 2).

So informal groups evolve over time. Your friends will probably influence the way you speak in some ways, though it's complex because you don't necessarily take on all of each others' ways of talking. The same processes can be observed in any group, though more formal groups may not have so long to develop nor such closeness. However, when people are brought together in teams, certain things have to happen if they are to be successful.

Question 13

Think about a good football team (or team from another sport). What is it that makes this group of people a team – that is, what are the qualities of a good team? How does this differ from the qualities of an individual athlete?

In many subjects at university there is an emphasis on group or team work. This is partly in response to employers' requirements for graduates who are able to work well with other people. Good team work exploits some of the advantages of informal groups that we have already seen; however, it can be tricky. We've already seen in the case study the problems faced by Anne because her 'team mates' avoided doing the work that was required.

Even the team that is made up of good friends can have problems with this – and there is a danger that it jeopardizes those friendships. The next extract from the case study illustrates the dangers and the steps that the students took to try to avoid problems.

Case study – 'we need a contract'

Khalid, Maria and Joe are in a team working on a project. They have to design something, write a report and make a presentation. They had each said that they would write something; Joe hasn't done anything yet. Maria is angry; Khalid thinks she is overreacting.

Khalid: We've still got loads of time, Maria – it doesn't help if you go off on one.

Maria: We'll get stuck if we don't keep it moving. It's not going to fit in with all the other stuff we've got to do. How do we know that Joe's going to do anything?

Joe: I will. It's just that it takes me a bit longer to write things because of my dyslexia.

Maria: OK, we maybe have to take that into account but they haven't given us any extra time, so we need to find some strategies to make sure it works. It's not just you, Joe. What Khalid's written just doesn't fit the topic anyway. . .

Khalid: I thought it was OK!

Maria: . . . and I'm not even that happy about my own bit. If we carry on this way, it'll be completely disjointed. But we do need stuff to work on.

Joe: I've done some drawings – it's just the writing I've got problems with.

Maria: These are great – why didn't you say so? But it's not what we agreed to do. But I think these would be a good starting point. Oh, what a mess. Where do we go from here?

Khalid: How can it be great and a mess at the same time? You panic too much Maria. Let's look at this calmly.

Joe: If I'm working on something, I need to know exactly what steps will be involved. And I need to know what to do if one step is missing. So I can see why you're annoyed, Maria. I would be as well if something was missing. But at the moment I don't know what it's missing from, if you see what I mean.

Maria: What we need is a contract. Khalid will do this, Joe will do that, I'll do the other.

Khalid: And penalty clauses?

Maria: Well, at least an agreement about how we can move on when bits are missing.

Joe: OK – let's try to work something out.

University activities 12. Group work

Quick note – now anxious student about letting team mates down and about general inadequacies in whole area

(extract from Christine's journal)

Group work can be a major cause of stress for new students. It is very difficult to work out what you should be doing when you are put in a group for the first time. In some courses, there will be some training in group work; in others, you are just likely to be thrown together and told to get on with it. On the following pages there is a template to help groups to establish a set of groundrules for a project. You may have to adapt this because of the particular requirements of your project. The key is to concentrate on *what has to be done*.

In my own case, I was concerned that I did not have as much engineering knowledge as my two fellow students and that I would let them down. (This type of fear can be common in some students.) However, when I thought about it, I realized I had a skill that they would probably welcome – report writing. They were quite impressed as I could quickly outline the main elements of the project report. In turn, one of my team mates was very good at putting together illustrations and the other was very good at calculations. (Of course, I should admit that this division of labour was probably not what was intended by the lecturer who set the task!)

We were lucky that we had such complementary skills; the important thing was that we had to talk to each other for a little while before we became aware of this. I think we all felt uncomfortable to start with, especially as we hadn't ever talked to each other before.

Other teams, though, have problems because more than one person thinks they have the necessary skills and they want to do it in different ways. I noticed this in the lab once.

I was with Simon and Ross who couldn't agree on method and level of detail. Simon wants to get on with it; Ross wants to be as precise as possible. He was also writing things down in a different sequence from Simon – he'd write down the error before he wrote the reading and this upset Simon who wanted a clear, logical approach.

(extract from Christine's journal)

Because Simon and Ross were friends, they didn't hold back when they disagreed with each other! I felt that we all learned through the types of argument that emerged during these discussions. It can be very frustrating, however, if you think you see what needs to be done and other people just won't go along with it. And it can be difficult to handle if you are still at the stage of being polite with each other and a 'group' way of talking has not evolved.

When things go wrong

Often the students I see who have got into difficulties have just decided to give up on the group work. However, it is important to note that even giving up is doing something that will have an effect on the final outcome (and probably not a good effect).

If things go really wrong, there are a number of steps you can try.

1 Look at the template in Figure 6.2 and work out whether you can adapt it for your current circumstances.
2 Call a 'crisis' meeting and outline alternatives – (a) this is what will

happen if we continue with what we're doing; (b) this is where we need to be.

3   Use assertive language and the language of negotiation – for example: By Thursday, we will . . . If you do . . . then I'll do . . .

4   Let the lecturer in charge of the class know what your problems are. It will sound better if you can propose a solution, for example:

George hasn't turned up at any of our meetings; he was going to cover the marketing issues. We have summarized the key points in a handout, but we haven't gone into any depth and we won't be presenting on this topic if he doesn't turn up. Will that be acceptable?

Students in context

Still on the theme 'you are not alone', it is important to recognize that there are many people around who will support, advise and represent you. It is useful to know who they are – and what they are called.

Sometimes American students are horrified to discover that there is a 'warden' in the hall of residence – to them that means a jailer. I hope they don't see me like that when they get to know me!

(warden at an ancient university)

Wardens in halls of residence are members of staff or students who live in halls and who are points of contact for anyone in difficulties. It is also their job to ensure that people comply with the rules of the hall and generally to ensure that things run smoothly.

You will find many people with this kind of role at university: acting as a go-between to ensure that everything is well-regulated and fair. They are your representatives: that is, they will make decisions on your behalf. In particular, there will be a group of people called something like the *students' association* or the *students' representative council*. They are the people who run the union for you.

The union

This body of students not only runs the students' union (a building) but is also your union that represents your interests to the university. In most universities, you are automatically a member of this union if you are a full-time student, though you can choose to opt out if you want.

Most student unions are formed of several layers. The following is a typical structure for decision-making (note that it may not coincide exactly with your own circumstances; I am just making general points here).

What is the group's main task?

Is a report required?   ☐

Is a presentation required?   ☐

What skills are needed to complete these tasks?

Writing   ☐
Design   ☐
Public speaking   ☐
Calculation   ☐
Drawing   ☐
Information gathering   ☐
IT skills   ☐
Interpersonal skills   ☐
Problem identification   ☐
Problem-solving   ☐
Other (list)   ☐

Who is in the group? How can they be contacted?

Name	Contact details

Can any of the key skills be associated with specific people?

What has to happen?

Tick any stages that are required for your group task. In the action column, put the initials of the main people responsible. Suggest a completion date for each stage. Add any other stages that are not included here.

Stage	Required?	Action	Completion date
Identify topic			
Identify required outcome			
Identify possible methods			
Agree method to be used			
Identify sources of information			
Gather information			
Perform experiment			

Create design			
Perform calculations			
Produce outline of report			
Write about method			
Write about findings			
Write background information			
Write conclusion			
Write introduction			
Edit whole document			
Produce illustrations			
Produce table of contents			
Produce references			
Proofread			
Prepare slides for presentation			
Decide on sequencing of speakers			
Rehearse presentation			
Hand in project			

Figure 6.2 Template for group work

All the students

They make decisions at the annual general meeting (AGM) or occasionally at an emergency general meeting (EGM). They also elect the *executive committee*.

The students' representative council (SRC)

They are elected from faculties or schools and make decisions about union policy. They meet several times during the year. The executive committee has to report to the SRC.

The executive committee (exec)

The exec is elected directly by the student body. Some of its members are on *sabbatical* – that is, they are full time and paid and have either taken time off from their studies or have just completed their degree. Some members are unpaid and part time. They all have different remits and titles, for example: president, vice president (welfare), vice president (commercial services). Some of the remits covered are likely to be: sports, clubs and societies, communications and publications, equal opportunities, advice and support – and there may be many others.

When we look at the student in the context of potential support, representation and advocacy (considering who will speak up for you), we find that the students' association or SRC plays a big part in the 'web' of support (see Figure 6.3.)

Support services

One of the difficulties in writing about support services in universities is that they vary so much between institutions. Again, the problem is largely to do with language – what the different departments and people are called.

Figure 6.4 lists just some of the services that can be difficult to find and are easily confused with other departments. The best way to find out what support is available to you is probably to go to your university's website and just wander around for a while.

The personal tutor

It is also likely that you will be allocated a member of academic staff who is your first point of contact for any concerns you might have. This person may then refer you on to the appropriate service department or person. Some of the names for this role, as well as personal tutor, are: academic adviser, adviser of studies, counsellor, director of studies, personal counsellor, regent, tutor.

As well as a range of names, there can be several different remits for this post: in one university, it might be a person who simply advises you on course choice; in another, it will be someone you can approach to discuss your personal circumstances. As lecturers move between universities, their own understandings of the role may be coloured by their previous experience, their own experience as a student and by the extent of

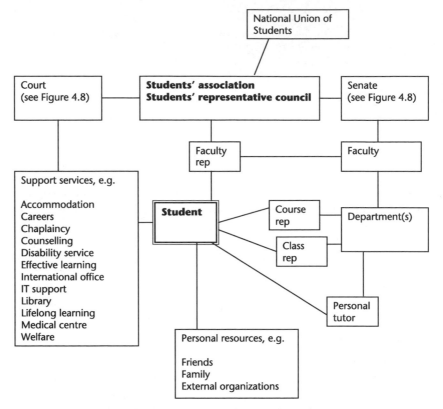

Figure 6.3 Organization chart for a university, showing the student in context

training they have received. Inevitably, some people are better at this role than others.

If you have been allocated such a person, it is very useful to try to see them early in the academic year to find out what exactly their role is. It is likely that you will have to contact them, for example, if you are going to miss any classes through illness or other problems.

Conclusion

This chapter has considered the wide range of people you might meet at university, including friends, colleagues, members of a team and people who can support you. The key issues raised here have been:

Type of Support	Look for...
How to study	Academic practice, academic skills, educational development, effective learning, learning and teaching, learning enhancement, learning support, study skills. There might be a centre, a department, a service or a unit offering such a service or it may be a single person – perhaps called adviser – in a support department with another title. Sometimes, the type of support you need can be found elsewhere. The university's library, for example, will have people who are very good at supporting you with finding and evaluating information
Financial problems	Student advisory, student financial support, student support, welfare, well-being
	There are often very distinctive roles for the department that collects money from you (fees, accommodation charges etc.) and the department that will help you with financial problems. So you may have a finance office (asking you for money) and a welfare office (helping you to find sources of money)
	You may also hear about: access fund, emergency aid fund, hardship fund
	There are usually two sources of advice about financial problems – one run by the students' association and one run by the university itself
Using a computer	Communications and information technology, computing services, information and communications technology, **information literacy**, information technology, learning resources, learning services, managed learning environment, technical support, virtual learning environment
	In many cases, the support service will contain an abbreviation of one of the above terms, e.g. C&IT, ICT, IT, **MLE**, VLE
	Often, libraries can advise on such support – and they will certainly be able to tell you where the help is located in your particular university
	Note that you should be careful not to confuse a department that teaches the subject of computing and a department that offers computer training. thus you might have in the same institution a department of computing (academic department) and a computing service (support department)
Being a part-time student	Continuing education, continuing professional development (cpd), credit transfer, distance learning, evening classes, lifelong learning, open learning
	You may also need to discuss part-time options with your own specific academic department, and seek advice from some other services (e.g. welfare)
	Most universities offer a range of options, including some courses that people just take for interest rather than a qualification. Some students opt for the part-time route for financial reasons, to fit in with working commitments

Figure 6.4 Support services

- We affect other people and are affected by them in what we do and say.
- It takes time to build up relationships.
- Sometimes you have no choice over the people you have to work with.
- You may need to develop skills of assertiveness and negotiation.
- Sources of support are not always obvious, and have a variety of different names in different institutions, but they will probably exist somewhere.

Students at university have many potential sources of support and representation – often more than they realize.

7   Real and virtual environments

Throughout the book, there have been some references to new technology and information technology (IT) and the language associated with them – for example, university websites, personal response systems, texting, electronic sources for lecture notes. This chapter pays special attention to new technology, but it is not a highly technical chapter. My concern, as in the rest of the book, is with the type of language you might encounter and how to respond appropriately to it. This applies whether you are a technophobe (someone who is terrified of technology) or a technophile (a lover of technology) or, like many people, somewhere in between.

Universities are places where there are rich technological resources, but it might not be what you expect, as illustrated by the following quotations.

I was kind of disappointed when I came here. I thought everything would be very high tech – but they only use the virtual learning environment to put up lecture notes. It means we have to print them out instead of being given photocopies. It's quite low level use of the technology.

(first year disabled student)

I'd found out about some *assistive technology* [see Glossary] at school, but I had no idea there was so much around that could help me. My friends are using some of it too – it's not just special needs.

(second year disabled student)

Some of these young students think they know it all because they've been playing with computers for years. This means that they don't listen, and the results show that they don't actually know it all.

(tutor for IT skills)

I thought it was all going to be about high ideas. I didn't think we'd be spending time learning how to wordprocess. Because I've never done it before, it's taking me ages. But it's not what I came to university for.

(first year mature student)

Whether you already very confident with IT or have never switched on a computer before, the chances are that you'll be changing some of your practices. Universities are changing too.

Universities are changing

Over the years, the requirements for attending university have changed. It is no longer the case that you have to be male, upper class and wealthy, for example. It is undoubtedly necessary to be able to read and write – to be literate – to benefit from university. In terms of language that you need to be successful at university, we have already encountered the notion of 'educated language'. Nowadays, it is also necessary to be *computer literate*, at least by the time you graduate. Indeed, you now need to use a computer to apply to university (see Chapter 5). Many universities now have a compulsory IT course, which you must pass before you can graduate. These are often the equivalent to (and sometimes the same as) the *European Computer Driving Licence* (ECDL – see Glossary).

IT can now be used to support most of the language use we have already considered. To take one example, the checklist of what needs to be done for a team project (Figure 6.2), Figure 7.1 gives just some suggestions about how IT might help. You might be able to think of others – e.g. using chat rooms, electronic discussion lists or *blogs* as sources of information.

You can see from the list in the figure how well IT can support and extend the things you have to do anyway. In some cases – such as preparation of a contents list – it can do something for you. A task has become so automatic that a machine can do it. You still have to identify the main headings in some way (perhaps by giving them a particular style) but the machine can pull them out and add the page numbers – tedious work that it is useful to automate.

Automation has changed a number of our key tasks, and subsequently the way we talk about them. The use of calculators, for example, meant that our ability to make a lot of calculations was greatly extended. But the extension of our ability can sometimes contribute to a decrease in knowing what we are talking about:

I get students who insist that the answer must be right because the calcu-lator says so. They expect the calculator to do the thinking for them as

Stage	How IT can help
Identify topic	There are special 'mindmapping' packages that can help you to explore initial ideas
Identify required outcome	
Identify possible methods	
Agree method to be used	If you are working in a group, then email or texting are very useful tools for keeping in touch and exchanging ideas
Identify sources of information	There are search tools on the Internet – the most famous one is Google (http://www.google.com). But you can also do searches on academic databases in your own subject area Check your library website. Your librarians should help you with this; it is part of their job so don't be afraid to ask
Gather information	Universities subscribe to electronic versions of journals, where students and staff can download articles free
Perform experiment	Much experimental work is now supported by computers or other sophisticated technology
Create design	There are packages that can assist design (CAD = computer aided design). There are different applications for different academic 'tribes'
Perform calculations	Spreadsheets can perform calculations for you. There is specialist software for different mathematical applications
Produce outline of report	Your wordprocessing package may have an outlining facility – check under *View*, for example, then scroll down and click *Outline*. Play around with the levels – or use the help facility to find out what it can do
Write about method	All students will be expected to use wordprocessing software to produce essays and reports
Write about findings	
Write background information	
Write conclusion	
Write introduction	
Edit whole document	Wordprocessing makes it possible to produce several drafts and make corrections easily

Figure 7.1 *continues*

Produce illustrations	It is possible to download illustrations from various sources on the Internet – for example, Google has a section devoted to images. You should acknowledge your sources for images as well as words
Produce table of contents	Your wordprocessing package may be able to create this for you automatically – for example, use *Insert* and then go to *Index* and *Table*. There are things you need to do to set up the table, however, e.g. use appropriate styles for your headings, or insert a marker where you want headings to be picked up
Produce references	There is software that can help you to do this. Some is quite expensive, but some is available free. Search for 'bibliographic software' on the World Wide Web for further information – and check your own university's website too
Proofread	Most wordprocessors have spelling and grammar checkers (though these need to be used with care)
Prepare slides for presentation	PowerPoint is a well-known package for preparing, storing, and running slides for presentation
Decide on sequencing of speakers	
Rehearse presentation	You can add notes to your PowerPoint presentation about any areas that are likely to cause you problems

Figure 7.1 How IT can help

well as the calculation. They have no idea what they are talking about – and sometimes they're talking nonsense!

(professor of mathematics)

When bits of what you are talking about can be automated, then it is important to be sure that you still know what you are saying. The same principle applies to use of the grammar checker. You shouldn't be changing something just because the grammar checker tells you to – you need to understand what it means. I often see students who blame the grammar checker for misplaced commas, but the final responsibility is their own.

The main message, then, is that you should be thinking about what the technology is telling you – not looking for a quick fix.

Some students just shove a word into Google and then incorporate into their assignment any old rubbish that comes up from their search.

(politics lecturer)

If you are using Google, you might want to ask yourself whose site you have reached. If it is the website of a pressure group, for example, they will have a very specific 'take' on a topic. You still might be able to use the information, but it is important that you recognize a possible source of bias. One student I talked to had been looking for evidence about smoking policy and had reached a section of the website of FOREST (Freedom Organization for the Right to Enjoy Smoking Tobacco), which campaigns against restrictions on smoking. She had not been aware of their stance and this made it difficult for her to interpret what they were saying and to realize that she was only getting one side of the story. While it was acceptable for her to cite their evidence, she needed to understand its context and the implications for her own work.

You should ask yourself the following questions about websites you intend to use for information:

- Is the site relevant for your own purpose? Are you clear what that purpose is?
- What do you know about the people who contribute to or host the site?
- Are facts or opinions being presented?
- Is the information presented from an academic perspective? This may not be necessary, but you should still know.
- Is there a potential bias in the information?
- Is the website mainly concerned with giving factual information or making money?
- How might academics regard this website? (This can be very difficult to tell, but it is worth asking the question.)

Websites and search tools provide a very useful way of accessing greater amounts of information, but you also need the ability to focus on the relevant information and to recognize a valid argument. So your ability to extend your information gathering must not happen at the expense of using your ability to reason.

Some current IT applications appear to go beyond extending some of our abilities – and take you to a whole new environment.

E-learning and virtual learning environments

The metaphor of another planet is a bit similar to the idea behind 'virtual learning environment' (VLE). You enter a special place where you will find information and can communicate with other people who have also entered that place. Some people don't like this term; they prefer to see VLEs as support for learning and think that the expression is confusing.

Some of the issues for students are raised in the next section of our case study. The University of the West of Scotland has decided to introduce a VLE –

at a time when three of our four students have never heard of the idea. The emphasis in this case study is not so much on the actual technology, but on how students might respond to the new language that they have to learn.

From my own experience this is a fairly typical conversation, though I have missed out the swear words and rude remarks about lecturers. As you read it, think about what you can say about the students' responses to something new.

Case study – life on a virtual planet

The students have all been given a handout explaining the university's new VLE and how their department is going to use it. The lecturer talks about it briefly at the end of the lecture and suggests that they 'log on to the VLE' as soon as they get the chance.

> *Anne*: What was all that about? I've no idea what a VLE is. Is it something we're going to have to do, cos if we don't I'm not going to bother.
>
> *Khalid*: And what's 'log on' mean? Look at this stuff – it's all initials and gobbledegook! As if we didn't have enough to do.
>
> *Maria*: You log on sometimes when you're using email. But is that the same? So will it be on your email?
>
> *Joe*: No not exactly. Though you can send emails from it. I've seen this already. The Disability Service showed me it – it looks OK. It'll be good for me cos the lecturers will be putting notes there so I can get them before the lecture. Supposedly.
>
> *Khalid*: So what's the point of going to lectures then if you get it all beforehand. Surely they won't do that. And put it where exactly? Is it a web page?
>
> *Joe*: Sort of. You go in through the intranet on to a site that has things you can download and places for discussion. And you can do tests and put stuff there yourself. But it's organized through courses, so there'll be one for our course that other people won't be able to see. I looked at it this morning – there's some stuff we've to fill in about how we see our personal skills.
>
> *Maria*: So we do have to use it. And there's homework there already. Sneaky.
>
> *Anne*: Does that mean everyone in the class can see what we think about our skills? Don't like that.
>
> *Joe*: Probably not. There's all sorts of different access routes – some bits only you and your personal tutor will see, apparently. Do you want me to show you how to get in?

Later on all the students have had a chance to look at the VLE. They meet the next day.

Anne: Well, I don't see myself using that much.

Khalid: You'll be going to the party though!

Anne: What party?

Khalid: Did you not see it in the 'chat' bit? That's the best bit.

Maria: The Administrator's already been in and told people to stop slagging lecturers off in the chat bit. I thought you said people couldn't see it, Joe.

Joe: The chat bit is open to everyone. And the Administrator does have special rights as he's got to sort things out if there are problems and make sure no one's doing anything they can be sued for.

Maria: Well, I thought it was OK and I liked the way I could get extra information. And it's like a place you can go to find out what's going on and do stuff for yourself. I've put my personal development plan on it already.

Khalid: You wee swot. So have I, mind you. I just wanted to see how it all worked.

Anne: Maybe I'll have another look at it. I didn't see half these things you're talking about.

Joe: There's some really cool stuff there – there's a great link to the Wikipedia and a suggestion we start something like that of our own.

Anne: [groaning] Now you've really lost me! One thing at a time please.

Some of the key points from this conversation are:

- When new technology is introduced, some people will find it intimidating.
- People sometimes think it will mean a lot of extra work (and they might be right!).
- It may seem to be an unnecessary innovation.
- It is useful to talk to others to throw some light on some of the terms used.
- Some terms may have been encountered in other situations (e.g. log on, in this case).
- Like Anne, you may not pick up all the possible functions and language when you first look at the technology.
- New methods and media will require new ways of doing things – for example, there may be more work for a different type of person (such as the administrator in the example above).
- Conversations like the above are very common and tend to move everyone's understanding about an issue on.
- It helps to keep an open mind about technology.
- Don't expect to understand everything immediately.
- Once you've got on top of one idea, there's likely to be another one around the corner!

I have used the idea of the VLE to illustrate these points, partly because it is current at the time of writing and partly because it is a bit similar to the metaphor of 'another planet' that I am using to consider language at university throughout this book. There are different names for VLEs – for example, there are commercial brands such as Blackboard or WebCT. There may be a VLE that has been developed within a university itself. If you want to find out more about VLEs, or their near relation MLEs (managed learning environments), you could try looking up 'MLE' on the Wikipedia at http://www.en.wikipedia.org/wiki/Main_Page.

Netiquette – how to avoid offending people online

If email or a VLE is used extensively by your academic 'tribe', then you will need to explore it. Don't worry about doing anything wrong; there are plenty of safeguards in it to prevent you from breaking it. But there are some things that can be said about polite use of electronic communication:

> One of my students keeps shouting at me in emails – she uses capital letters all the time. I don't think she means it, but she probably doesn't realize what effect it is having.
>
> (lecturer)

> I can't stand it when they write 'hi' in their messages to me – I keep thinking, I'm not your pal; I'm the person who's going to be marking your essay.
>
> (lecturer)

> We do discourage flaming (using insults online) as it quickly gets out of hand.
>
> (VLE administrator)

'Netiquette' (network etiquette) is a topic that may change several times over the lifetime of this book – as things develop, new forms of politeness emerge. You can find various websites offering advice about it. It's complicated by the context it is in too – here we're not only thinking about general politeness on the Internet, but also about university life. So rather than being specific about not writing in capitals etc., I'm encouraging you to think about how do other people using this particular way of communicating get their messages across? For example:

- What kind of language does the lecturer use or avoid using?
- How informal are people? For example what kinds of greeting are used (hi?, dear . . .)?

- What sort of names are people called (first names, family names, nicknames)?
- Are there any abbreviations, slang, swear words? It's probably a good idea not to use any of these if you are not sure.
- Is there any use of emoticons (pictures to show emotion), for example a 'smiley' :) made up of punctuation marks? (Even if this acceptable, it's usually best to keep it to a minimum.)
- How is humour used in communications? Are there people from other cultures or backgrounds who might find this humour offensive?
- What do your emails and other online communications say about your relationship with the other person?
- What do their replies say about their relationship with you?

Question 14

How do you feel about the list of netiquette considerations? Do you think you should modify your 'electronic' language for different circumstances? How similar is this to modifying your face-to-face language?

Universities are changing

It's worth repeating that universities are changing; they no longer conform to the types of institution you might see in old novels and films, for example. But the changes go beyond that. Because universities are in the forefront of technological development, both within the tribes themselves and with respect to university teaching, it is likely that your own university will change during your time there. It is useful to be aware of this and also to attempt to keep track of it. If a change is happening at university while you are there, your experience might be of great interest to potential employers and others once you have left.

Checklist for technology

During your time at university, you will probably need to do some or most of the things in the list in Figure 7.2. Because universities are changing, there will be things omitted from this list and you may want to add them as you encounter them. The main aim of this list is to make you aware of the language associated with certain things you are expected to do so that you have the right words available to ask for help if you need it.

While items in the checklist in Figure 7.2 are essential for students at

Activity	What this refers to	Done?
Visit the university's website	This is the public face of the university on the Internet. Once you are a student at the university, you are likely to have access to other parts of it – the **intranet** – either through university machines or through a password	
Fulfil the university's IT requirements	Many universities have a test (e.g. ECDL) for students to complete either before they start or before they graduate. It is likely to include use of wordprocessing, spreadsheets and databases	
Know your own university email address	Most universities now have email addresses for all their students. If someone needs to contact you quickly, this may be their preferred method. Even if you like to use another email address, you should be checking your university one as well	
Use the library's catalogue	University library catalogues are now in electronic database form. You will probably be able to access the catalogue from the university's website, especially if you are on campus. If you don't know how to use this, ask your library's help desk or information service Don't be embarrassed about this; it is part of their job to help you	
Get and use an **Athens account**	You'll find out more about this from your university library. An Athens registration and password gives you access to electronic journals. This is particularly important for **postgraduate** students, but it's also useful for **undergraduates**	
Know how to access and use the university's VLE	This is a space on the Internet where your department may keep most of its information, make most of its communications and expect you to participate	
Find your department(s') website	Most university departments have websites or pages on the university's website that contain important and useful information	

Figure 7.2 Checklist for technology

university, there will be some other changing aspects of the language that I have been unable to anticipate. These could include:

- new ways your academic 'tribe' works and therefore speaks, writes and makes other forms of communication;
- new academic tribes with their own languages;
- more cross-disciplinary work so that the idea of tribes or disciplines disappears;

- new effects of international collaboration, resulting in new language and cultural practices among students;
- new technologies not yet known about.

It is not the technology itself that is responsible for the new language, but the way it interacts with our existing practices and cultures. If you are interested in this topic and would like to read more about it, there are some suggestions in the Bibliography.

Conclusion

You are entering university at a time of rapid change in what we do and how we talk and write about it. However old your university is, it is unlikely to use language in exactly the same way as it did when it was established – though the influence of its older ways of speaking and writing may still be apparent. By the time you graduate, it will probably have changed again and you will be a contributor to and part of that change. The Glossary at the end of this book will probably soon need a whole new set of words to keep it up to date.

Afterword

A guidebook can only take you so far – the rest of it is up to you. But there is a strong message that I want to end with, on behalf of all our universities. Universities depend on people to continue their work and existence. They especially depend on students. Once you have joined a university, you are a part of it and you will make a difference to it, however small.

You are very welcome on our planet.

Glossary

The glossary indicates some words that have been used in the book and a few others that you might hear frequently. The definitions are not as complete as you would find in a good dictionary; I am concentrating on likely uses for new students. You are advised to purchase a good dictionary presented in a style that suits you and that is likely to be useful for your subjects.

Note that some examples in the column 'You might hear . . .' will not necessarily apply in your own institution. I have tried to pick typical examples, but all institutions have their own ways of saying things!

(n) = noun
(v) = verb
(a) = adjective

If no letter has been used, then the word is a noun. See Figure 5.14 for a description of parts of speech.

Word	Definition	You might hear. . .
abstract	(n) a summary of a document	Read the abstract of the journal article to see if it is relevant for your essay.
	(a) existing only as an idea or concept (as opposed to *concrete*)	'Force' is an abstract idea; you can't actually see it but it is a useful way to describe relationships between objects.

Word	Definition	You might hear. . .
academic	(n) a person who is studying or teaching, usually at a university (a) scholarly	You need to get your interlibrary loans request signed by an academic. Academic writing is different from journalism.
academic tribe	a metaphor for a group of academics who work in the same area	You probably won't hear the expression 'academic tribes' at all, but I have used it extensively in this book to mean the lecturers and other people involved in your subject area, particularly thinking about how they use language.
acronym	a word formed from initial letters of a phrase	'CHESS' is the acronym for the Coalition of Higher Education Students in Scotland.
admissions officer	a person who approves a student's application to a course, usually a lecturer in the relevant department or faculty	You should speak to the admissions officer for the department about whether your qualifications meet the entry requirements.
adviser of studies	a person allocated to a student to advise on academic life; there are various other possible titles (see Chapter 6)	Your adviser of studies must sign your course selection document.
aegrotat	an archaic word meaning medical certificate or degree granted when the person was ill (rarely used)	Before an aegrotat degree can be awarded, the registrar must receive appropriate medical and academic evidence.
analogy	a comparison between two things that highlights similarities; often the simpler being used to aid understanding of the other	The analogy between the computer and the human mind breaks down when we take the effect of emotions into account.
argument	a line of reasoning (see Chapter 5)	All essays should have a clear argument.

assignment	a piece of work to be submitted as part of a course – it could be an essay, a report, a set of short answers, a solution to a problem, and many other things (see Chapter 5)	The course will be assessed by one exam (60 per cent) and three assignments (40 per cent).
assistive technology	technology used to support the completion of a task, often associated with disability; examples include voice recognition technology, predictive technology (where the package anticipates which word you are trying to write)	You must alert the department if you will require the use of assistive technology in an exam.
Athens account	a subscription to a service that allows you to access academic journals electronically	You should enquire at the university library about how to gain and use an Athens account.
bibliography	a list of works referred to in the process of writing an essay or other work; this includes works not specifically cited	We do not need a bibliography for your essay, just a set of references.
blog	a web-based publication (originally web log) a bit like a diary, consisting of a number of articles usually in reverse chronological order	If you are referring to blogs in your research, you must be very careful to distinguish between fact and opinion.
canon	a list of books etc. that people believe should be standard reading (this is controversial – see the answer to Question 4)	Feminists sometimes argue that the canon is simply a list of books by dead, white males.
case study	1 a story used to illustrate some key principles 2 a history of a particular institution or person 3 an assignment based on analysis or interpretation of one of the above	The tutorial will be based on the case study in the textbook. You should read it and think about the main principles that are evoked.
chair	1 a professorship	A new chair in entrepreneurship has been announced.

Word	Definition	You might hear...
	2 the person presiding over a meeting	Each student will take a turn of acting as chair and secretary of the committee.
chancellor	the titular head of the university – i.e. the person who has the formal title, but does not actually do the day-to-day work; this is different in some US universities, where the chancellor is the working head of the institution	The chancellor will give the closing address to graduates and guests at the end of graduation.
citation	the act of quoting from another person's work	Students must acknowledge their citations in the body of the essay as well as in a list of references at the end.
clearing	the final process of allocating places to students on university courses, undertaken after firm offers have been accepted and allowing students to have been unsuccessful to gain an available place on another course	If your exam results were not as good as you expected, you can possibly still find another course or another institution through clearing (see UCAS website).
collusion	working with someone else but passing off the resulting work as one's own (see Chapter 5)	If two identical submissions are received, it will be assumed that collusion has taken place and both students will held responsible.
computer literate	(a) competent in the use of a computer, possibly to a specified degree	Students who are not computer literate will have to undertake an additional course.
concrete	(a) real, material, able to be experienced (as opposed to *abstract*)	There was no concrete evidence of any weapons of mass destruction.
counsellor	1 a professional person qualified to offer advice, especially with personal problems	The counsellor offers a free confidential service for a variety of personal issues.

	2 a person who has been assigned to particular students to be a first point of contact for advice. The former is usually in a service department and the latter in an academic one (see Chapter 6); some universities also offer academic qualifications in counselling	You should see your academic counsellor at the start of each semester.
court	the governing body (administrative) of some universities (compare with *senate*)	The university court has approved the expenditure for a new sports centre.
critical incident analysis	identification and exploration of a significant incident, episode or a problem; it is particularly used in reflective practice, where a person thinks about what happened, why it happened, what they have learned from it and how they might do things differently – it does not have to be a negative event	You are expected to make a critical incident analysis of at least one event that occurred during your placement.
dean	the head of a faculty; the role is frequently a temporary one, undertaken by a senior academic for a specific period	The dean will address all new students during induction.
demonstrator	a person who demonstrates experiments in a science lab, and possibly helps students to perform their own versions	Check your calculations with the demonstrator before you make the final adjustments.
diet	a period when exams are taken; the term is particularly used in Scottish universities, but can be seen in others too	If you have a medical certificate, you may be able to take the resit exam as a first diet attempt.
direct entry	the process of coming into university at the second or third level on the basis of qualifications gained elsewhere; it is also sometimes used as an adjective – a direct entry student	If you have an HND, you may be able to gain direct entry into third year at some universities.

Word	Definition	You might hear. . .
discipline	1 an academic subject or field of study 2 punishment for infringement of regulations; 'academic discipline' is sometimes a heading in a set of regulations	Books in the library are organized by academic discipline. If students fail to hand in work, they may be subject to disciplinary procedures.
dissertation	a lengthy piece of writing, usually based on research and putting forward a thesis; it sometimes refers to a piece of work that is a particularly long essay; it is more likely to be required of postgraduate or final year students than first years	Students are required to submit a dissertation proposal in the first semester and then the complete dissertation by the end of the academic year.
Dr	the title for a person who has achieved a medical degree or a PhD	The lecturer should now be known as Dr Sinclair as she has been awarded her PhD.
dyslexia	a condition affecting about 10 per cent of the population that results in difficulties in reading, spelling or writing; it has a number of possible causes and effects; it is also frequently associated with compensating abilities, for example in creativity; the condition does not relate to a person's intelligence	A diagnosis of dyslexia is made by an educational psychologist, who will also make recommendations about appropriate strategies and support for the particular student.
ECDL	see *European Computer Driving Licence*	
e-learning	a general term that refers to learning that uses electronic support, such as a VLE or web materials	Many students like the flexibility of e-learning; staff prefer the emphasis to be on the learning rather than the e!
enrol	(v) to join the university; see also *matriculate* and *register*	Students in second and third year may enrol by post or online.

e-portfolio	a collection of evidence of progress kept in electronic form; it may include a personal development plan (PDP)	Assessment will be by submission of an e-portfolio, which should contain your best pieces of work, your reflections on it and a set of guidelines. (Note that what an e-portfolio actually contains can vary considerably.)
essay	an essay is a fairly short piece of writing often used in universities to check students' understanding of a topic and ability to write about it; see Chapter 5 for advice on how to write essays	A good essay has a beginning, a middle and an end. The beginning sets out what you're going to do, the middle does it and the end concludes that you have done it.
European Computer Driving Licence (ECDL)	a certificate that shows its holder has reached a particular level of competence in a range of computing packages	Holders of the ECDL are exempt from having to do the IT literacy course.
evidence	something that indicates, supports or proves a belief or fact	Hard evidence might include witness statements, statistics, expert opinion, experimental findings (and there are many other possibilities).
executive committee (exec)	the governing body of a students' association or students' representative council, elected by all the students of a university (see Chapter 6)	The exec meets this week to discuss the problem of increased prices in the union.
extension	permission to hand in an assignment later than required	Extensions are not usually given in this course; late submission will result in deduction of marks.
external examiner	an appropriately qualified person from another university who checks that the assessment of the courses is undertaken fairly; the external examiner scrutinizes the marks and will see all or a sample of the exam papers/assignments	The marks are provisional until the external examiner has seen the scripts.

Word	Definition	You might hear. . .
faculty	in the UK, a grouping of departments in a university; in the US and some other countries, *faculty* refers to academic staff	Students from the Faculty of Arts should attend induction on Wednesday morning. If you do not know which faculty you are in, you should check the website.
feedback	in terms of assessment, a response that provides information and guidelines to help you make improvements (see Chapter 4 on responding to feedback) 'feedback' is also used in some technical subjects in relation to the return of the output of a system to the input – and this is where the above definition comes from	Don't just look at the grade for your work – read the feedback as well to ensure that you improve or maintain your high standard.
first diet	see *diet*	
fresher	(n) first year student, usually just referring to those in their first few weeks at university (a) belonging to first year	Freshers will find lots to do during Freshers' Week at the Union. At the Freshers' Fayre, there will be all sorts of attempts to get new students to join different clubs and societies.
glossary	a list of frequently used or specialized words, usually presented in a similar way to a dictionary	If a frequently used textbook has a glossary, then these are words you may want to know and be able to use.
graduate	(n) a student who has achieved a degree (compare *postgraduate* and *undergraduate*) (v) to leave with a qualification *graduation* is a ceremony to celebrate the achievement of a degree	You need to be a graduate nowadays to be considered for many jobs (see also the end of Chapter 6 for what people say about graduates).

graduate teaching assistant (GTA)	a postgraduate student who helps with teaching	The tutorials will be led by a GTA.
handbook	a manual to explain the things you are most likely to need to know – many university departments or courses have a handbook and staff get very frustrated when students do not read them	You should check the handbook before you begin your assignment – there may be some useful guidance.
head of department	senior academic in charge of a department; service departments also have heads of department; in both cases, this is the person to speak to if you cannot sort out any problem	Students who are not happy with the way their courses are run should contact the head of department in the first instance.
hypothesis	a possible explanation to be put forward and tested	It is necessary to look for evidence that will support or refute your hypothesis.
index	an alphabetical list of subjects dealt with in a book, usually with corresponding page numbers and usually at the end of the book	If you're looking for a definition, it's often a good idea to look in the index and go to the first mention of the subject.
induction	a period of introduction at the beginning of a course of study; it often coincides with freshers' week and enrolment but they are separate processes	During induction, you will meet the lecturers and receive information about support departments in the university.
information literacy	the ability to find, evaluate and use information effectively	Too many students use the Internet indiscriminately; more attention to information literacy is needed to ensure that they can find good quality information.

Word	Definition	You might hear. . .
institution	an organization (in this context, for education) or the building housing it; several institutions offer higher education, including universities, colleges, art schools etc.	Every institution has its own way of doing things, but some institutional practices can be very mysterious to outsiders.
Internet	a computer network of digital information	If you have Internet access at home it may help you with your studies.
intranet	an internal Internet, with access only allowed from particular machines or via a password	Once you have enrolled as a student, you can use the department's intranet.
jargon	specialized language used in a particular subject	The textbook contains so much jargon that students find it hard to follow initially.
journal	1 a publication that appears regularly that looks a bit like a formal magazine and contains academics' papers on the latest findings in the subject	The latest edition of the academic journals are on display in the library; some journal papers can be downloaded from the Internet.
	2 a diary or day-book that contains a record of what you have done	You are expected to keep a journal about your studies during the first semester.
lecture	a talk on a particular subject, usually academic; a lesson (see Chapter 4 for advice on attending lectures)	It is useful to think about the topic before you go to a lecture; it prepares the mind.
lecturer	a person who gives a lecture; a title for a university teacher	There are five lecturers in the department, each with a different specialism.
literature review	1 the process of reading as much as possible about a particular topic	You should do a literature review before you reach any conclusions about this question.

	2 a written account of the key issues and principles of a topic as covered by the writers in the subject; it is often presented near the start of a thesis or article to provide a context for the author's own contribution	A dissertation will include a literature review as well as your own work.
Master's degree	a higher level degree, usually taken after a first degree; however, some first degrees have now been expanded so that they include Master's degrees	Students often start a Master's degree before deciding to embark on a PhD.
matriculation	the process of becoming a member of the university by enrolling	You will need your matriculation card to join the library.
metaphor	a figure of speech where a thing is called something else that it resembles	The book *Understanding University* uses the metaphor of another planet to consider alienation at university.
mindmap	a non-linear form of notes, where the main idea is placed in the centre of a page and all the themes and subthemes branch off from it (see Figure G.1)	If you make a mindmap of your lecture notes or of a chapter of a book, you are processing the information – summarizing it and finding connections.

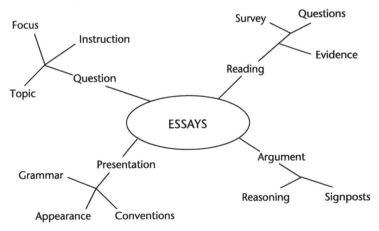

Figure G.1 Mindmap

Word	Definition	You might hear. . .
MLE	managed learning environment see *virtual learning environment*	
open day	a day when people can visit a university and talk to representatives about courses they might be interested in	There's a job for students to help show people around at open day and tell them about university life.
paper	1 an essay or article that might be submitted to a journal or read at a conference or seminar	Each student will be expected to prepare a seminar paper on one of the lecture themes.
	2 a set of exam questions	You can find the past exam papers in the library.
participle	an incomplete form of a verb; there is a present and a past participle	The present participle is the form of the verb ending -ing (going, being, planning etc.).
past participle	the past participle is generally formed by adding -ed to the verb but there are many exceptions to this (see Chapter 2 for one problem with past participles)	The past participle is used to make the passive voice – for example: The experiment is planned for tomorrow.
PBL	see *problem-based learning*	
PDP	personal development plan (sometime professional development plan); a record of what has been achieved and what you intend to achieve over a particular period of time (see Chapter 5)	In some places, the PDP portfolio is a piece of assessed work.
person	in grammar, 'person' refers to who or what is speaking, is spoken to or is spoken about: *first person*: I, we *second person*: you *third person*: he, she, it, they, or a noun, e.g. the professor	In many subjects, students are expected to write only in the third person.

personal response system (PRS)	a system of voting using hand-held remote devices that activate a sensor.	Using the PRS is a bit like being on *Who Wants To Be a Millionaire*, but it makes you concentrate on what the lecturer is saying!
personal tutor	a person – usually an academic – whom a student sees to discuss issues affecting the course of study (see Chapter 6)	Students are expected to see their personal tutor once a semester to discuss their personal development plan.
PhD	doctor of philosophy; a higher degree, usually entirely research based; the holder is entitled to be called Dr; there are other degrees that lead to doctorates and some of them have a taught element	A PhD student will frequently do some undergraduate teaching as well.
plagiarism	representation of someone else's work as one's own, sometimes defined as academic theft; it can include taking someone's writing and changing a few words in it (it is mentioned several times in the book, but see especially Chapter 5)	The best way to avoid plagiarism is to close the book and write in your own words what you think the author is saying. It is also important to correctly reference the sources you have used.
postgraduate	(n) a student who already has a degree and is taking a higher degree, diploma or certificate (a) relating to such students or their work	A postgraduate course can provide a useful preparation for a specific job.
principal	the head of the university	Students see their principal when they arrive at university and when they graduate.
problem-based learning (PBL)	an approach to teaching where students are expected to make their own investigations into authentic problems in the subject; it is now often found in courses related to medicine but also in other courses (see Chapter 5)	In a PBL class, there are sometimes no 'right' answers but decisions are still required.

Word	Definition	You might hear. . .
professional body	a collection of professional people that determines how the profession should be regulated; a number of professional bodies set out requirements that university courses have to meet; some notable examples are the General Medical Council and the General Teaching Council, but there are many more	The professional body requires to know whether students are likely to be 'fit to practise' by the end of their course.
professor	in the UK, this is the title of a person who has reached the highest grade of an academic position; the title can be associated with a *chair*, in which case, the person who gets the post that is called a chair automatically becomes a professor; for some other staff, the title is a personal one, given on merit; the usage contrasts with that in many other countries, where any lecturer might be called professor and their title is assistant professor, associate professor or full professor	The department has a new visiting professor (a person who holds the title for the duration of the appointment).
project	an assignment that involves both study and doing something, usually requiring a report; quite a loose term that can refer to many different activities – either to do by yourself or with other people; it often involves several stages, including a planning stage where you outline what you are going to do	It is a good idea to check any departmental handbooks for project guidelines.

prospectus	a publication showing what is on offer at a university, particularly its courses but also describing social life and other aspects of the environment; usually a glossy marketing document, designed to highlight the best features of a university, but it should contain accurate information about courses, dates in the academic year etc.	If you phone up the university, they will be happy to send you a prospectus. They may ask you if you want an undergraduate or postgraduate one.
pro vice chancellor	a person who acts on behalf of the vice chancellor and often has a very specific role in the university (see also *vice principal*)	The pro vice chancellor for teaching and learning has asked all faculties to ensure that their students understand the policy on plagiarism.
reader	the most senior lecturer grade (between senior lecturer and professor)	The senior lecturer was promoted to reader on the strength of her extensive research in her area and publication in highly regarded journals.
reason	(n) justification, explanation, cause, motive; the mind's ability to draw conclusions (v) to give a reason, to infer, to argue, to set out logically	You must give reasons for your opinions and conclusions. If you can reason effectively, you will have mastered one of the principle uses of language at university.
referencing/ references	acknowledgement of the books and other works consulted in a piece of writing; various approaches to referencing: for example, author–date (Harvard), author–number (Vancouver); your department may well give you guidelines for referencing; it is a good idea to check any handbooks you are given; if you are told just to be consistent, then it can be helpful to follow the style of referencing used in one of your textbooks	New students have a lot of problems with referencing at first; it can be very confusing because there are so many possible styles and different staff seem to have different preferences.

Word	Definition	You might hear. . .
	typically, there is a reference within the text itself and then a list of full references at the end of the document references may be direct or indirect (see Chapter 5, especially the section on avoiding plagiarism)	
register	(v) to enter one's name in a list of members of the university or a specific course in it; the process of registration may also be referred to as enrolment or matriculation	In some universities, students enrol with a faculty and can then register on different courses of their choice; at others, they register for a full course.
	(n) the tone and formality of a piece of writing relating to the circumstances in which it is used; students should generally be aiming for an academic register, rather than, for example, a journalistic one	The student was marked down for inappropriate register; the lecturer had felt that the style was too informal and chatty for an academic essay, even though the content was accurate.
registrar	literally, the person who keeps the register; in a university, the registrar is a person who holds a senior administrative position and is responsible for ensuring that proper records are kept (if you are doing a medical degree, the title *registrar* has another meaning relating to a grade of doctor)	The registrar has stipulated that valid medical certificates must be presented at the time when a student misses an exam.

registry	the offices of the registrar; this is usually quite a big department and the work is likely to be allocated into faculties or schools; if you have to take documents to this department, you may be asked what faculty you belong to the department that processes enrolments, exam results and graduations; it also ensures that the university's regulations are followed	Students who enrol late will have to take their documentation to registry.
regulations	the rules of the university; all universities have regulations to ensure they run smoothly; some will affect you more directly than others, especially to do with exams and coursework (see Chapter 5)	The regulations say that students are not allowed to have copies of their exam papers after they have been marked.
report	a factual document, usually commissioned by someone to investigate and report back on a particular issue (see Chapter 5 for the difference between an essay and a report); you might find yourself reading reports as well as writing them	Students are expected to read and comment on the report of the enquiry as part of the research for their essay.
research	(n) an investigation aimed at increasing knowledge on a topic maybe in response to a question or problem or to test a hypothesis all university students engage in research, even if it is simply reading a textbook to find out the key point (v) to make such an investigation	You are expected to undertake a piece of research into one of the following topics. . . If you research your topic fully, then you will be able to identify what the principal writers said about it.

Word	Definition	You might hear. . .
researcher	a person who devotes a considerable amount of time to research; this might be a student (often then called a research student) or someone specifically employed to research into a particular problem a researcher might also be known as a principal investigator and be in charge of one or more research assistants	A researcher has sent out questionnaires to a number of students to find out how they are coping with university life.
resit	(n) an exam that is taken again, usually because it was failed the first time (v) to take such an exam; it is also sometimes necessary to resit coursework (a) descriptive of such practices e.g. the resit coursework will be posted out to you in July	If you have a resit, then it is likely to take place in August. The regulations state that a student may resit the exam only x times (often two or three). In both exams and coursework, the resit exercise might be either different or the same as the original. It is advisable not to make assumptions about this, but to find out.
sabbatical	a period of leave when a lecturer or student undertakes another piece of work – in the case of students, it refers to the year that a student takes up a paid post in the students' association or students' representative council	When the student president completes his sabbatical year, he will return to his studies. Some presidents like to get their degree first before taking their sabbatical – it is still called this, however. But they do have to do it immediately after they graduate.
scare quotes	inverted commas, either single or double (' ' or " ") used to show indicate some doubt about a term or to suggest that this is not a conventional usage; they should be used sparingly (and some people say they should not be used at all)	Students who use too many scare quotes in their essays can give the impression that they are doubting their findings.

they have been used occasionally in this book, especially in Chapter 2 with respect to 'educated' language.

scholar	a serious student; an educated person	Scholars have disputed the authenticity of the text.
scholarship	1 scholarly learning	The international exchange visits are designed to promote scholarship and collaboration.
	2 a financial award to allow someone to study	Many students are unaware of the range of scholarships available that will allow them to study.
school	1 a group of university departments, usually for administrative purposes	Universities keep changing their structures and we find that instead of four faculties, there are now seven schools (or vice versa).
	2 a group of people who hold a common view of a subject	The behaviourist school of psychology is radically different from the cognitivist.
secretary	the title for two very distinctive jobs	
	1 a person in a department who attends to the clerical work and may well be a good source of information about regulations and procedures; sometimes students are expected to hand work in to a departmental secretary	If you have been absent from a class for medical reasons, you should hand your certificate in to the secretary.
	2 a senior person in the university management who is appointed to write or transact business for the university; this person will deal with legal issues	The university secretary has discussed the university's contribution to the student union with the student president.

Word	Definition	You might hear. . .
semester	an academic term, originally referring to a half year course (from the Latin words for six months); most universities have two semesters a year, but some now have a third one over the summer	The first semester continues after the Christmas break (at least, in some universities).
seminar	a discussion between a group of students and a tutor; sometimes, a seminar paper is provided by one of the students (see Chapter 4 and also *tutorial* as these two words are frequently interchanged)	Students are expected to read specific material before each seminar so that they are in a position to contribute to the discussion.
senate	the governing body (academic) of some universities (compare with *court*)	Senate has approved the principle that all students are entitled to support with their personal development planning.
senior lecturer	a lecturer who has been promoted because of various achievements, probably particularly with respect to research	One of our senior lecturers will take the first seminar as she is an expert on the topic.
signpost	(in essays) a word or phrase that shows where you are in the argument e.g. firstly, secondly . . . (see Figure 5.7)	Your essay jumps about too much; I'd like some signposts that say: 'Here is the problem and here's how I am going to try to solve it.'
structure	how something (here language) is organized, particularly with respect to form, function and meaning; a sentence structure (usually) has to have a main verb and a subject; the structure of an essay contains a line of reasoning sustained through the beginning, middle and end (see especially Chapter 5)	Students often complain that lecturers don't explain what they mean by 'weak structure'. It may refer to grammatical structure in sentences or to the overall structure of the essay. The reader needs 'signposts' to see why you are writing what you are.

student	a person who studies; a person who is enrolled at a university; these two are not necessarily the same thing – but they ought to be! (see Chapter 6 for some comments on student identity)	Some people find that it takes time to get used to the idea of being a student – it has an effect on the way you see yourself.
students' association	the body that represents students and provides various kinds of support and commercial services; you are usually automatically a member of the students' association of your university, but it is possible to withdraw if you do not want to be	The students' association has an annual general meeting which all students are encouraged to attend.
students' representative council (SRC)	the representative body for students that may be part of a students' association or be the name for a group with a similar function	The SRC is recruiting for representatives in each faculty.
suspension	usually, exclusion from university for breaking regulations; it can also refer to an interruption or delay to the studies that might be requested by the student (sometimes known as 'voluntary suspension')	After the plagiarism came to light, the student was suspended from the university for a semester.
syntax	grammatical structure in sentences that contribute to the way we make sense of them; you might also see 'syntactical' the word is often used adjectivally in the expression 'syntax error', which has a specific meaning in computing, but which is also to do with permitted constructions	Lecturers often remark that students have poor syntax, and the students do not know what they mean. It usually means that the student has not constructed sentences properly (for example, using incomplete sentences or running them together). Often when there are syntax problems, it is because the student is trying hard to say things in an academic way but without plagiarizing, and they are not yet familiar with how such written sentences work.

Word	Definition	You might hear. . .
technician	a person employed by a department to do technical support; for many science subjects, technicians are involved in setting up and supporting labs; there may also be technicians who provide audio visual or IT support	If you need access to the lab, you should contact one of the technicians who will tell you when it is available.
tense	the form of the verb that indicates time (in this case, we're not looking at the meaning associated with stress, either mental or physical, we're considering the grammatical meaning)	It can sometimes be difficult to decide whether to write in the present or past tense; the main advice is to be consistent.
text	1 a book or other piece of writing, now extended to other forms of communication such as drawings	The set text for this course will be available on short loan (3 hours) in the library. It is recommended that you buy your own copy.
	2 the words used in a piece of original writing (as opposed to translation, for example)	If we pay close attention to the text, we shall see how the language changed.
	3 the language used in sending messages between mobile phones and similar devices	Tutors do not like to receive 'text speak' in emails and, especially, essays.
	in some subjects, the word 'text' will have an additional very specific technical meaning: for example, religion, history, or computing. (see Chapter 2)	
theory	an explanation put forward to bind together knowledge of the world in a meaningful way – often associated with abstract ideas or contrasted with practice	Undergraduate students are usually expected to comment on established theories, or attempt to apply them, rather than come up with any new theories of their own.

thesis	1 a lengthy piece of writing based on original research, especially associated with PhDs and other doctorates	The thesis should be over 70,000 words but should not exceed 100,000. (The lengths vary from one subject to another – this is typical of an arts or social science PhD thesis, but even within those subjects there may be differences.)
	2 a theme or position adopted for argument and to be defended against attack (unlike a hypothesis, where you may decide to reject the position)	If your thesis is defensible, then it should not be possible to find any counter examples.
tutorial	small group teaching session – originally one-to-one – where the student is coached or instructed by the tutor; nowadays, because classes tend to be much larger, tutorial is frequently another word for seminar	You can be suspended from the course for missing tutorials.
UCAS	University Central Admissions Service; the body that processes applications to UK universities (see Chapter 5) if you are applying to a university in another country, you will not go through UCAS	The UCAS admissions process begins in autumn; it is important to check their website for details.
undergraduate	usually, a student who does not already have a degree or a word applying to a course that such a student might be taking, in just a few cases, students without degrees will be enrolled on postgraduate courses and they would then count as postgraduate students; when used as an adjective the word undergraduate specifically refers to the level of the course, but it is used to talk about people too	Undergraduates today often have to combine paid work and study.

Word	Definition	You might hear. . .
university	a place of higher learning that has the power to grant degrees; there are frequently disputes over any further definition (especially what 'higher learning' might mean) the word derives from the Latin for 'whole'; originally the word emphasized the gathering of teachers and students, rather than the building, and some people would still rather think about a community than a place	In a university, you are expected to think for yourself, not just to regurgitate what you are told.
university secretary	see *secretary*	
vice chancellor (VC)	the head of the university (compare *chancellor*), a bit like the chief executive of a company; sometimes (especially in Scotland) this role is known as principal and in some universities the same person will have the title 'principal and vice chancellor' (usage varies in other countries too)	The vice chancellors of the UK universities have all expressed concern over, e.g. funding, university buildings, student preparation for university, completion rates. . . . if VCs comment on something, it's usually a very important issue.
vice principal(s) (VP)	a person who stands in for the principal; some universities have more than one VP, in which case they will probably look after a particular issue, e.g. research or teaching and learning in some universities, the term pro vice chancellor will be found	The vice principal for teaching and learning has asked for a survey to be undertaken about why some students leave university without completing their studies.

virtual learning environment	a site accessed through the university's intranet where a variety of information and activities are stored; if it is called a managed learning environment (MLE) it suggests that there is an integrated system involving registry and other functions in the university it means your details of enrolment, attendance, and exam success can be accessed as can anything you have put on it yourself, such as a portfolio of coursework there are strict controls over who has access to different parts of these sites; some universities develop their own; others use commercial ones such as Blackboard or WebCT (see Chapter 7)	If you check on the VLE, you'll be able to access last year's exam papers, the student handbook and the suggested reading for the first essay topic. You should also participate in the email discussion that has been started there. (There are many potential uses of the VLE – the above just offers some of the more common suggestions.)
VLE	see *virtual learning environment*	
warden	a person with responsibility for students staying in university accommodation; this person lives in the accommodation (see Chapter 6)	Students sometimes have to ask the warden to intervene when their neighbours are too noisy at night.
welfare	1 a state of doing well, especially being financially secure 2 a department, frequently part of a student advisory service, that deals with financial issues and general student well-being; the students' association usually has a welfare rep as well	Welfare advice is available through an appointments system. It covers many issues, e.g. what happens if your student loan does not arrive, dealing with difficult landlords, balancing your budget. If you have any financial worries, you should approach the university's or the union's welfare team.
wiki	a web application that allows users to add or edit content	You can find out more about wikis in the Wikipedia: *http://www.en.wikipedia.org/wiki/Wiki*.
World Wide Web	a collection of pages and links that can be accessed on the Internet	The 'Web' is changing the way we work, think and communicate.

Appendix: comments on questions

Question 1

Can you think of any expressions you use with your own group of friends, your partner or your family that other people might not understand? Or an expression that you would only know if you'd seen a certain TV programme?

There are many possibilities for this. Fans of the books about Harry Potter will know what you mean if you talk about muggles (people who are not wizards), but others might not. If my husband asks me if I've seen his 'gorgonzolas', I know that he is referring to his tracksuit trousers – no one else could possibly be expected to know this! And if an 'educated' person says: 'Curiouser and curiouser', then they're not just using poor grammar; they are deliberately quoting from *Alice in Wonderland* by Lewis Carroll.

Question 2

What sort of texts are you likely to study at university? Think about their age, the reasons they have emerged, how they were written or produced. Have they changed over time and are they likely to change much in the near future?

Your answers will of course depend on the subject you will be studying. You are very likely to use books, whatever that subject is. In many subjects, you will be expected to use the latest edition of a book so that you have the most up-to-date information. When I studied philosophy, I had new editions of some ancient texts – and also modern commentaries on them.

One person I studied was Plato who wrote down many of the dialogues of Socrates. Socrates himself did not approve of the written form of language – he thought that meant that people would no longer 'practise their memory'. Without Plato's writing it is possible that Socratic dialogue would be lost to us forever.

Question 3

Imagine a very correct older person trying to speak the language of young people in your part of the country. What would they sound like? Would they be able to do it? What would need to happen before they could do it properly?

Often when older people try to mimic the language of the young they get it wrong in subtle ways. A few years ago, I was surprised to hear young people say 'That's pants!' when they didn't approve of something. I didn't ever use the expression myself – I thought it wouldn't sound right coming from me. When I was young and an older person said: 'Of course, I'm just an old square,' I remember thinking: 'Yes, you are – especially if you use the word "square". Nobody says that now!'

By the time an older person has encountered the word, it may well be out of date. They also often get the context wrong. An older person who does use young people's language confidently has probably spent a lot of time with the young and knows exactly when it is the right time to use a particular word.

Sometimes new students feel in a similar position to an older person trying to be young – like a fish out of water. But it is a different situation; getting a degree does mean changing the way you use language. With any change in language use, you need to see or hear the word in context a few times. But it's OK to risk a bit of ridicule if you are going to start using the language – you'll never find out if you've got it right if you don't try it out.

Question 4: What language do you encounter?

Consider your own exposure to educated and powerful use of English. Is it already quite high? Could it be increased? Think about what happens in the circumstances given in Figure 2.3. Note that it is not being suggested here that you should give up the reading, cultural activities or friends you enjoy! However, it may be possible for you to increase your exposure to some of the alternatives. How far do your answers in the two columns coincide?

Figure A.1 shows some examples of the preferences of some 'educated' people. There are many other examples; these are just to give you a flavour (and may also reflect some of my own prejudices and preferences). There is also much dispute about this kind of thing – what should be in the *canon* (see Glossary)? The point of this exercise – and much of Chapter 2 – has been to alert you to these types of debate and the judgements that people might make about you on the basis of your knowledge about what they regard as 'essential' reading. You don't have to accept their views, but it is useful to know about them.

Newspaper	*The Guardian, The Daily Telegraph*
TV channel	BBC2, BBC4
Type of programme	Documentary, drama
Radio channel	Radio 3, Radio 4
Type of programme	Documentary, humour, classical music, drama
Books	Classics – e.g. by Jane Austen or Charles Dickens; modern classics – e.g. by James Joyce, Doris Lessing, A.S. Byatt, Iain Banks (I've just picked out a few)
Children's books	*Alice in Wonderland* and *Through the Looking Glass* by Lewis Carroll, *The Narnia* series by C.S. Lewis
	Currently perhaps the *His Dark Materials* trilogy by Philip Pullman might be valued. A lot of people read the Harry Potter books and they are certainly a point of reference. There are many others
Music	Classical, jazz, blues – and a huge range of popular music. It certainly helps to have some knowledge of popular classical music – for example, Bach, Beethoven, Mozart
Discussions with friends	Politics, current affairs, religion, ideas. But many 'educated' people do talk about football and celebrities as well!
Internet sites	Search engine – Google *http://www.google.com* (but see warnings in Chapter 7 about its use) Academic journals – Athens *http://www.athens.ac.uk* News sites, e.g. BBC *http://www.bbc.co.uk*
	There are many other sites that have useful information. One of the skills you'll have to learn at university is how to discriminate between poor and good quality information

Figure A.1 'Educated' preferences

As well as the issues asked about, you might also want to think about films, plays, exhibitions and other cultural activities that are likely to help increase your vocabulary and knowledge.

Question 5

Can you think of any local uses of grammar or vocabulary that seem to differ from what the 'educated' people say?

This of course will depend on where you come from. Figure A.2 contains some further examples.

Dialect example	Standard English
I were going to London.	I was going to London.
We was going to London.	We were going to London.
Innit?	Isn't it? or Is it not? (or omit altogether)
You ain't seen nothing.	You haven't seen anything.
Here's the play what I wrote.	Here's the play that I wrote.
I have gotten my exam results.	I have got my exam results.
(except in the USA where 'gotten' would be Standard American English)	

Figure A.2 Dialect and standard English

Question 6: Identifying readers and purposes

In Figure 2.5, there are four pieces of writing. You may notice that two of them are written in more neutral language than the others. There are other observations you might make about the language as well. You're asked to say something about reader, purpose, and writer. Comments on this exercise are at the end of the book.

These four very different examples of writing were all written by the same person – who has also written the book you are reading. I often use this exercise to demonstrate to students that you can – and must – change your style of writing when you have different readers and purposes in mind.

Number 1 is an extract from a story entitled 'I Can't Stop Loving Him' in a teenage magazine written in 1979 (Blue Jeans, published by D.C. Thomson). Although it is written in the first person, it is not actually true. Notice how short the sentences and even the paragraphs are. In fact, the sentences are not strictly grammatically correct: 'A married man, naturally,' does not have a verb. The language used is emotional and personal and is meant to sound like a young person speaking aloud. This is a very appropriate style for this type of journalism; sometimes I have had to tell students that it is not so appropriate for academic writing.

Number 2 is an extract from a report I wrote when I studied mechanical engineering to find out about being a student again. It uses neutral language and the conventions of report writing, such as the expression 'terms of reference', which means a statement about the purpose and scope of the report and who commissioned it. You can also see a reference to a book by Deming – at the end of the report the full details of this book are provided in the References section.

Number 3 is an extract from the *literature review* in my *PhD thesis* (see Glossary for the meanings of these terms). Because it is referring to a lot of books, you can see the names of the authors and the dates of publication in brackets. The author's name only goes in brackets if it is not a necessary part of the sentence. Notice how I bring the ideas of a lot of authors together to make my own point. This is very common in academic writing. I have made reference to a specific page (85) for Daniels to acknowledge that this is where I got the importance of the expression 'unit for analysis'. Some of the uses of words in this are specific to my own subject area: e.g. activity, signs, mediate, mediated action, register, genre.

Number 4 is an extract from an open learning training course I wrote for London bus drivers in 1987. The company, London Buses, was introducing new one-person operating systems for buses and wanted to raise awareness of some of the customer care issues that would arise. This particular section is part of a response to an activity where readers were encouraged to think of advantages of the new system. The language had to be direct: not time-wasting, but not patronizing either.

Question 7: The language of your textbooks

Take two textbooks that you will be using this year, ideally as different as possible. See whether you can answer the questions in Figure 3.1.

I have completed this exercise (see Figure A.3) because I don't believe in setting people questions I am not prepared to answer myself. I chose two books from my Master's course on language and literature in the social context. Of course, I have already read these and in my notes I am trying to compare my actual reading with the impression I remember having before I started. Book A is Holmes, J. (1992) *An Introduction to Sociolinguistics*. London, Longman, and Book B is Fairclough, N. (1989) *Language and Power*. London, Longman.

	Book A	Book B
Is it going to be easy to read? Why?	It looked long (over 400 pages) and I also thought I might find references to many different countries confusing. But it looked well organized so I thought it wouldn't be too difficult	The contents page showed that the word 'discourse' would be used a great deal and so would the idea of 'critical language study'. This did suggest it might be difficult – perhaps 'heavy', but I was interested. In fact, I did find it quite challenging, but there were many useful 'signposts' as the author demonstrates how his argument unfolds
Is the language formal or informal? What examples show this?	Some of the examples of language use are very informal. But there is clearly a lot of jargon about language – e.g. the word 'diglossia' was a bit intimidating – but in fact it means the varieties of language 'high' and 'low' that I have been discussing in this chapter	The author uses the first person and tries to write directly to his readers (he states this early on). But there is a lot of jargon, some of which I struggled with
Does the book seem to value: • clear argument? • real-life examples? • illustrations? • problem and solutions? • theories? • other?	It particularly values real-life examples of language in use and it emphasizes variation. It is itself concerned with values as they are reflected through language	It particularly values theory and also a procedure for analysing the way we speak
Does the book have an index at the back? Are there words in this that you don't know yet?	There are fewer unfamiliar words than I might have expected. Looking up diglossia shows that it's mentioned in various places in the book. It has a useful glossary	The index has a lot of abstract ideas and also mentions a number of authors that I had not heard of and one that I had already had problems understanding
What does the contents page tell you about the way the book is organized? (e.g. does it build up a story, deal with several separate issues, move from simple to complex ideas?)	It's in three broad sections, with an introductory chapter. It was useful for me to recognize these broad sections when I started to read it	It shows a build up from theory to practice with a final chapter thinking about the implications
What other features are there in the language of these books?		I became aware early on of a sympathy with the author's political views, which helped me want to read the book

Figure A.3 Comparison of textbooks

The point of this exercise was to encourage you to engage with the books before reading them. I probably usually look at books with some of these questions in mind; it helps to prepare the mind for what is to come. If it looks particularly difficult, then I know I'm going to have to find a strategy to get what I need from it.

Question 8

Have you forgotten any important expressions represented by the Greek letters in Figure 3.3? Might you need them for your university course?

There are many possibilities and they vary from subject to subject. Here are just some uses for the lower case version of the letter we have already seen.

σ (lower case sigma)   divisor function (number theory)
standard deviation of a population (statistics)
sigma factor of RNA polymerase (biology)
Stefan-Boltzmann constant of radiation (physics)

If you are doing a mathematical subject, you might find it useful to check the entry for 'Greek letters used in mathematics' in Wikipedia. This can be found at http://www.en.wikipedia.org/wiki/Greek_letters_used_in_mathematics.

Question 9

What do you think lecturers are looking for in an essay?

I gave the answer to this question in the text immediately following it in Chapter 5. When I ask students this question, they do usually come up with some aspects of the four answers given:

1 answer the question;
2 show evidence of relevant reading;
3 have a good line of reasoning (argument);
4 present the essay well, following academic conventions.

Occasionally, people will say that lecturers are looking for knowledge or understanding. This is probably true, but what is particularly important is that it is *relevant knowledge*. Sometimes students think that they have to put everything that they have been taught into an essay, and that leads them to present a lot of irrelevant information.

Question 10

How is a report different from an essay?

Again, there are comments in the text immediately after the question. However, the question is perhaps not as straightforward as it might seem. Some lecturers will say that headings and subheadings only belong in reports; others quite like them in essays too. Sometimes departments avoid the issue by asking students to complete an 'assignment', and it is up to you to think about how structured it should be. Perhaps a useful way of distinguishing essays and reports depends on whether you are building up a carefully reasoned answer (essay) or marshalling a number of facts from which you are going to draw a conclusion (report). Ask for guidance from the department if it is not clear – if there is an expected format then following it is part of the assignment instruction.

Question 11

What do you think Anne's answers to the questions might be?

Here are some suggestions.

- *What do I want to happen?*
  To get the project started. For us to agree who is doing what. To be able to discuss how we might a good mark.
- *What (if anything) am I prepared to do in return?*
  Draw up an outline. Create a list of tasks. Start the research.
- *What does the other person want to happen?*
  Have some fun. Postpone starting the project.
- *What am I willing to concede (to give up or to allow to happen)?*
  To do a little bit more than is fair. To start by myself. To spend some time with the others, but more on work than socializing.
- *What am I not willing to concede?*
  Just doing enough to get by – I want a good mark. And I don't want to go to the party or generally hang out with these two.

Question 12

At the end of the encounter, Anne feels relieved. She has got what she wanted. What techniques did she use?

She used some standard assertive negotiating techniques:

- a firm statement of what she would and would not do;
- a repetition of what she would not do when Kate tried to persuade her (sometimes known as the 'broken record' technique because you just keep repeating the message until it is heard);
- a clear statement of what she expected from the others;
- use of the formula 'if you . . . then I . . .';
- making sure that the other people involved would gain from the approach.

Question 13

Think about a good football team (or team from another sport). What is it that makes this group of people a team – that is, what are the qualities of a good team? How does this differ from the qualities of an individual athlete?

Members of a team are all working towards the same goal, but they may take different roles in pursuing it. So the division of labour is important. It is a good idea for a team to play to individual strengths where possible. It can be useful to have someone who is willing to take a lead, but this will not necessarily always be the same person or the person it's supposed to be! It is actually better to have a mix of personalities; too many similar 'types' can get stuck.

It is important for each member of the team to be clear about what they should be doing and how they relate to other members – who is going to pass the ball to whom? This may mean it is necessary to explore some possible approaches.

These points show that there are things that have to be done (using language) that relate to the task in hand and also things that have to be done to look after the team and its communications.

Question 14

How do you feel about the list of netiquette considerations? Do you think you should modify your 'electronic' language for different circumstances? How similar is this to modifying your face-to-face language?

One big difference between electronic communications and face-to-face language is that electronic communications are closer to writing and therefore can be 'heard' over and over. So if someone is offended by it, the evidence can be there for longer. Because it is a new hybrid form (a mix of written and spoken communication) and because there is so much electronic communication, rules have sprung up quite quickly. They are frequently broken, but people do get very offended when that happens. As with any communication, you get more from the encounters if you consider its effect on other people. You are more likely to achieve your purposes if you think about your audience/ readership.

Be particularly careful about who you send the email to. Many people have been caught out by sending a personal email to a whole group, especially when they are using a discussion list.

References

The following references are to books specifically cited in the text that I have not covered elsewhere, for example with an acknowledgement or in the example of an essay. This is to give readers sufficient details to find the books themselves if they want to. You are likely to have to provide a similar list for your own writing at university.

Becher, T. (1989). *Academic Tribes and Territories: intellectual enquiry and the culture of disciplines*. Milton Keynes, SRHE and the Open University Press.

Clanchy, J. and Ballard, B. (1997). *Essay Writing for Students: a practical guide*, 3rd edn. NSW, Australia, Pearson Education Australia Pty Ltd.

Cottrell, S. (1999). *The Study Skills Handbook*. Basingstoke, Macmillan Press Ltd.

Fairclough, N. (1989). *Language and Power*. London, Longman.

Holmes, J. (1992). *An Introduction to Sociolinguistics*. London, Longman.

Sampson, K. (2003). *Freshers*. London, Vintage. (NB: contains strong language and sexual scenes)

Wilby, P. (2005). Restore Bog Standards, *The Guardian*, 28 July.

Bibliography

There are a few themes touched on briefly in the book that people might want to follow up in more depth. The following titles may be of interest, but you are encouraged to look for some of your own.

Brown, J.S. and P. Duguid (2000). *The Social Life of Information*. Boston, MA, Harvard Business School Press.
Why IT may change universities, but won't get rid of them altogether (among other interesting topics)

Buzan, T. (2003). *Use Your Head*. London, BBC Books.
The latest version of the original 'mindmapping' book

Cottrell, S. (2003). *Skills for Success*. Basingstoke, Palgrave Macmillan.
What to think about for personal development planning

Covey, S. (1989). *The 7 Habits of Highly Effective People*. New York, Simon & Schuster.
Inspirational ideas that will help you to communicate

Creme, P. and Lea, M. (1997). *Writing at Univeristy: a guide for students*. Buckingham, Open University Press
A practical guide focusing on specific writing tasks

Goleman, D. (1997). *Emotional Intelligence*. New York, Bantam Books.
There is more to a successful life than IQ

Levin, P. (2004). *Write Great Essays*. Maidenhead, Open University Press.
Levin, P. (2004). *Sail through Exams*. Maidenhead, Open University Press.
Levin P. (2004). *Successful Teamwork*. Maidenhead, Open University Press.
A growing series of accessible study skills titles

Mercer, N. (2000). *Words and Minds*. London, Routledge.
How we use language to think together

INDEX

Related books from Open University Press

Purchase from www.openup.co.uk or order through your local bookseller

WRITING AT UNIVERSITY
A GUIDE FOR STUDENTS
Second Edition

Phyllis Creme and Mary R. Lea

- What is expected of you in university writing?
- What can you do to develop and build confidence in your writing?
- How can you address the variety of written assignments you will encounter in your studies?

Writing at University is a student writing guide with a difference. It provides a deeper understanding of what writing at university is all about, with useful methods and approaches to give you more control over your academic writing.

The book explores both traditional essay and other kinds of writing that you will need to do as part of your studies. You are encouraged to build upon your existing abilities as a writer through applying practical tasks to your own work.

The second edition of this best-selling title has been completely updated with new coverage of report writing, learning journals, electronic writing and using the internet.

This book is an essential tool for anyone who wants to improve their writing skills at university or FE colleges, including both undergraduates and postgraduate students. It is key reading for students in courses that require essay, report, or dissertation writing and for students returning to study. It is also an invaluable resource for academic staff who want to support students with their writing.

Contents
You and university writing – First thoughts on writing assignments – Writing for different courses – Beginning with the title – Reading as part of writing – Organizing and shaping your writing – Putting yourself into your academic writing – Putting it together – Completing the assignment and preparing for next time – Using different kinds of writing – Using learning journals and other exploratory writing – References – Index.

160pp   0 335 21325 1 (Paperback)

STUDENT FRIENDLY GUIDES
SUCCESSFUL TEAMWORK!

Peter Levin

This short, practical guide is for students who find themselves placed in groups and assigned a project to carry out.

- Allocating work appropriately
- Dealing with people who are taking a 'free-ride'
- Resolving disagreements
- Working constructively with people who they don't like very much.

The guide helps students to appreciate the tensions between the demands of the task, the needs of the team and individual's needs, and to understand why people behave as they do in a team situation. It provides reassurance when things get stressful, and helps students learn from the experience and make a success of their project.

Contents
Part One: Basics and Context – What do we mean by 'a team'? – The benefits of working in a team – Teamwork skills – Academic teamwork and the job market – Part Two: Getting Started – Get in your groups – Get to know one another – Formulate your ground rules – Check out your assignment and plan your work – Part Three: How are we Doing? – Progress on the project – Progress from 'group' to 'team' – Personal progress – Part Four: Perspectives on Team Behaviour – Tensions: the task, the team and the individual – Team roles – Management systems and team organization – Team development: forming, storming, norming, performing . . . – The decision-making process – Negotiation – Cultural traits and differences – Individual traits: 'cats' and 'dogs' – Part Five: Teamwork Issues and Solutions – The task: getting the work done – Personal and inter-personal issues – Part Six: Benefiting from the Experience – Getting feedback – Reflection – Applying for jobs

136pp   0 335 21578 5 (Paperback)

STUDENT FRIENDLY GUIDES
SAIL THROUGH EXAMS!

Peter Levin

A must for all students preparing for traditional exams!

This lively, short and to-the-point guide helps students prepare for exams in which they have two to three hours to answer a number of questions which they have not previously seen.

Written in a straightforward and supportive style, this guide:

- Enables students to take control of learning and revision
- Cuts through academic obfuscation
- Explains the language of exam questions

It provides a range of techniques and approaches which students can tailor to their own personal circumstances.

Practical, down to earth and on the side of the student, this invaluable resource helps all students to achieve their very best in exams.

Contents
The strange world of the university. READ THIS FIRST! – Introduction – Part One: Using past exam papers – Get hold of past exam papers – What to look for in past exam papers – Unfair questions – The guessing game: What topics will come up this year? – Part Two: Formulating model answers – What are examiners looking for? – Interpreting the question – Methodology – Materials – Drawing up a plan – An alternative approach: the 'question string' – Choose your introduction – Argument or chain of reasoning? – Writing exam answers: some more suggestions – Questions for examiners – Part Three: In the run-up to exam – Revising effectively – Memorizing – Make best use of your time – Getting in the right frame of mind for exams – Part Four: On the day of the exam – Be organized

112pp   0 335 21576 9 (Paperback)

HOW TO BE A STUDENT
100 GREAT IDEAS AND PRACTICAL HABITS FOR STUDENTS EVERYWHERE

Sarah Moore and Maura Murphy

This exciting guide is perfect for all students, especially those new to higher and further education.

How to be a Student helps tackle the challenges and opportunities associated with life at university and college. 100 actionable ideas, strategies and tactics help you to make the most of your time, including:

- Turning up to your lectures and what to do while you're there
- Knowing what plagiarism is and learning to develop belief in your own voice
- Making presentations with confidence and style
- Being more creative
- Spotting signs that you need to take a break
- Dealing with boredom
- Preventing small obstacles from becoming big problems
- Not letting money issues get in the way
- Remembering that people once thought that Einstein was a slow learner
- Treating your CV as a working document

And much more!

Drawing from the real experiences of students, this book presents ideas and suggestions that you can use to enhance your time at university and to improve the quality of your learning life.

2005   208pp   0 335 21652 8 (EAN: 9 780335 216529) Paperback   £12.99

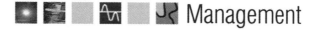